DID I... MY WAY
and
YOU *CAN* TOO

BY AL AUSTIN

How I parlayed lessons learned growing up on a farm in Virginia and a BS degree from a Historically Black College into a senior level executive position at a major US corporation

Published
By

UBUS COMMUNICATIONS SYSTEMS
26070 Barhams Hills Road - Drewryville, VA 23844
(434-378-2140 - www.khabooks.com

SECOND EDITION - FIRST PRINTING
January 29, 2015

FIRST EDITION - FIRST PRINTING
December 1, 2015

Copyright © 2015 by Alfred Austin. No part may be legally reproduced without the permission of the copyright holder or the publisher: UBUS Communications Systems, P. O. Box 1, 26070 Barhams Hills Road - Drewryville, VA 23844.

ISBN# 1-56411-656-5   YBBG#0654

The Author, Alfred Austin is a national Motivational Speaker. He is also available for consultation and book signings.

PRINTED
IN
UNITED STATES OF AMERICA
Post Office Box 1 - Drewryville, Virginia 23844
434-378-2140

DEDICATION

This book is dedicated to my mother, Rena Austin Taylor. Without her foresight, guidance, tenacity and caring, none of this would have been possible.

FOREWORD

There are few people you meet in life who seem to just know what's important in a situation. Few who have a clear sense about how to make things better, how to see through the fog and grasp what should be done. There are few who when they see a problem, will take it upon themselves to fix it; have the courage to say and do the things that everyone else knows they should have said but didn't. There are even fewer who do this and make you smile and admire their passion for life and who overcame great odds to get to where they are. Al's motto seems to be, "The world is not perfect. Ok. Fine. I can make it better."

Al's rural farm upbringing, strong family and desire for education set the foundation. But it was his desire to make things better that, in my opinion, sets his career apart. Al learned early in life to change things and to challenge the wrongs. Whether it was as a young boy questioning a surgeon who thought his arm needed amputating (turns out it didn't), sleeping on his mattress in the middle of a field at night to protest university policy (it got changed) or arguing toe-to-toe with his own CEO, Al believes you can make a difference.

Al pursued making things better by studying, setting a vision and goals, and working hard. He first applied these ideas to himself. He read books by experts throughout his career to stay ahead and be prepared; he worked hard, and believed in himself. One of my favorite quotes from the book is, "You can get people to do almost anything if your motives are pure, your rationale convincing and sincere and the interaction takes place in an atmosphere of trust and mutual respect." Al applied that to his life and to his career, even surviving a corporate witch hunt while growing his unit's revenue by 3000%!

In a world where executives are focused on big data, global regulatory changes, driverless cars, the internet of Everything, and disruption of every kind, Al reminds us that the fundamentals are still important. Fundamentals such as getting the workforce engaged, changing the culture, believing in people, treating people with respect, and not accepting the status quo. Read Al's story and challenge yourself to make a difference.

Paul L. Walker, Ph.D., CPA
James J, Schiro/Zurich Chair in Enterprise Risk Management
Executive Director, Center for Excellence in ERM
St. John's University

INTRODUCTION

In more than 40 years in business I have always been amazed at the lack of common sense that exists in most corporate environments. Values and behaviors that we learn early in life and expect from our interactions with others suddenly become so elusive that tremendous amounts of energy and resources are expended in a fruitless effort to recreate them in a corporate culture so hostile that they have no chance to develop. Trust, Candor, Reliability/Accountability are encouraged, rather than expected. Diversity is so feared and misunderstood that it often requires a senior-level executive to oversee its introduction into the discussion and then has no chance of achieving its intended purpose of providing the different perspectives that are crucial to the imagination and creativity necessary for a striving business. Any mention of Empowerment has been known to send seasoned professionals running for the hills. Risk Taking, once the hallmark of progressive companies, has all but disappeared from the lexicon of most organizations. Setting High Expectations is seen as such a threat to reporting good results that mediocrity has become the acceptable level of performance at every level of the organization. Today when corporate executives discuss Employee Engagement, there appears to be a complete lack of understanding, not only of what it means, but also, and more importantly, what it takes to achieve it. The prevailing idea is that employees control their level of participation with no regard for the leadership style or culture they work under. Without enlightened leadership, that expects candor, inspires trust and insists that decisions are made by the most knowledgeable and free-thinking people in the organization, employee engagement will not happen and companies will continue to underperform.

This book is about my life. While I acknowledge the natural tendency to embellish events of the past, I assure you that what's depicted here is true and accurate to the best of my ability.

I encourage you to enjoy the stories, but focus on the message/learning. If you do, you will see how, with the lessons learned from growing up in a large family, on a farm and a BS degree in History and Government from a Historically Black College, I could compete against some of the brightest minds in business, with advanced degrees from the best business schools in the country, and WIN.

This book is about seeing your uniqueness as your greatest strength and not an obstacle to your success. It is about knowing your limitations and being comfortable with them. It is about leadership and followership. It is about courage, confidence, self-esteem and succeeding against all odds. It is about effective communications never being out of style; that it's as important to listen as it is to speak; that it is almost impossible to convey passion and emotion with sound-bites; that passion and emotion are important ingredients in your success; that Twitter, Facebook, Instagram and Texting are not substitutes for face-to-face dialogue. It is about embracing diversity as a cultural imperative, understanding that different perspectives are the life-blood of successful organizations. Albert Einstein once said; **"No problem can be solved from the same consciousness that created it"**.

The following pages will chronicle my almost 30 year career with a major U S corporation. It will detail my rise from trainee to senior vice-president in an environment that was not always friendly, but ripe with opportunities for those willing to challenge the status quo. You will learn that holding on to the values and behaviors we acquire to maintain our personal and family lives are just as important and effective in organizations. You will learn that Fun, Excitement, Success and making a major contribution are not mutually exclusive, but a critical combination for achieving your dreams. You will learn that, **if your motives are pure, your rationale convincing and sincere, and the interaction takes place in an atmosphere of trust and mutual respect, you can get people to do almost anything**. You will learn about the **FIVE P'S** to success and how this dynamic formula will propel your career forward. You will learn the **Four Traits** all great leaders must have and the **Six Characteristics** of high performing organizations. You will learn how to achieve **Employee Engagement** at a level that will significantly improve performance and employee satisfaction; **"that the productivity gains realized from the invention of the microchip, pale in comparison to the potential of a fully engaged workforce."** Finally, you will learn that Leadership, whether on a personal level to achieve your individual goals or as the Chief Executive Officer of a major organization, is not rocket science, its common sense.

THE BEGINNING

I was born on January 12, 1948 at Southside Hospital in Farmville, Virginia, the seventh child of John and Rena Austin and the first boy, after six older sisters, Cassandra, Muriel, Doris, Lottie, Joyce and Irma. My father, the teacher in the local one room school and a Baptist minister, in Cartersville, Virginia was a prominent member of the community, so my arrival was a really big deal. He graduated from Virginia Union University in 1925, and his diploma is one of my most-prized possessions. I have often wondered what motivated him to pursue a college education at a time when a Black man with a college degree was a rarity and must have required a tremendous sacrifice to achieve. Unfortunately, I never got to know my father. I was two when he died in 1950, at the age of sixty.

In 2011 one of the churches my father had pastored contacted my sisters and asked that they provide a portrait of him to hang in the church. We enlarged a nice picture and had it framed. The church asked that we attend a service to present the picture. We prepared a program where two of my sisters spoke and one of my nieces read a poem. I acted as emcee. Halfway through the program, standing in the pulpit where my father had led his congregation more than 60 years prior, it occurred to me to ask the audience if anyone present had been a member of the church when my father was pastor, thinking that was not likely. A couple stood up, and the gentleman proudly announced that, "Not only were we members of the church then, your father married us 62 years ago". I was stunned. It was one of those magical moments that will stay with me the rest of my life and provided a connection to my father that I never had before.

When I was five-years old, my mother remarried, after

11

having been left alone to raise seven children. I am still astounded that someone would take on that responsibility, but my mother was an amazing woman, and I'm sure my step father, Richard Taylor, like my father, 27 years older than she, recognized that. I have always believed that one of the reasons Richard married Rena was to acquire an instant seven-person work force. And work we did. A successful farmer with only a third-grade education, he owned 125 acres of land, on which we grew everything from vegetables to tobacco. He had dairy cows and raised chickens and turkeys for the A & P Tea Company, at the time, one of the largest grocery store chains in the country. We also sold milk to A & P. I use to say the only thing I learned from working on the farm was that I did not want to be a farmer. But as I realized later, on the farm I learned values and beliefs that have served me my entire life.

Raising a large family in the segregated south, in the 50s and 60s was a tremendous challenge. My mother taught us that we were responsible for each other and our home. We were not allowed to let anyone intimidate or degrade us or any member of the family. The way we carried ourselves was important in maintaining the level of respect we expected from the community. Honesty and Trustworthiness were cornerstones of my mother's messages. Being dependable, courteous and staying out of trouble were reinforced on almost a daily basis. My mother clearly understood that avoiding compromising positions was a key to maintaining our safety. Respect for authority was not demeaning, but a critical part of good citizenship, required of everyone. She insured compliance with a disciplinary policy that none of us wanted to face. She also practiced what she preached; she walked the talk.

She and my stepfather were among the most respected people, Black or White, in our community. Miss Rena, as she was known by many, was smart, caring, generous and ready to provide assistance to anyone needing it. While race was certainly a factor, she instilled in all of us that it did not define who we were or what we could accomplish. That would be the result of our intellect, our character, confidence and a willingness to work hard. She taught that racism was the other person's problem; we should work to eradicate the ignorance that drove racist thinking, but we should never let it interfere with the achievement of our dreams. So when at age eight I announced that I wanted to be the first Black president of the United States, she didn't laugh or mock me, she said "if you aim for the moon and miss and land on a star, you will have accomplished a great deal".

The village of Cumberland, the county where we lived, had the white-only water fountain and one segregated restaurant. Whites dined in the front where Blacks were not allowed. Blacks were served through a window in the rear. Rena would not allow us to eat there, and we all understood why. It wasn't until Prom night of my senior year in High School that I and three friends and our dates, dressed in tuxes and evening gowns, marched in the front door of a place I had never been inside. We were seated without incident and served. I never set foot in the restaurant again. Interestingly, our visit didn't cause a stir or any lengthy discussion that I'm aware of. It was almost as if it never happened. I'm not sure why. It did make me wonder why we hadn't walked in the front door before.

The school system was completely segregated with separate schools for both elementary and high school students. Cumberland was one of the neighboring counties to Prince Edward County, where in 1959 all public schools were closed rather than integrated. They would remain closed for five years.

1955 was an eventful year for our family. First, on May 3rd my stepfather took my mother to the hospital to give birth to her eighth child. Coincidentally, May 3rd was Richard's 65th birthday. On May 5th my brother, Richard Mason Taylor was born. To say that my stepfather was thrilled would be a gross understatement. Though he already had a daughter by a previous marriage, having a son was the realization of a lifelong dream. I was also excited to have a baby brother, even though I was now no longer the youngest family member. Since I was now seven years old, and mature beyond my years, sharing the limelight with Mason, as we called him, was a joy. Richard lived to be 98, and saw Mason grow into manhood.

The second big event of 1955 was my oldest sister Cassandra's graduation from Virginia Union University. We all celebrated this accomplishment, made all the more special because my father had graduated from there 30 years prior. She earned a degree in education, and her first job was math teacher at Luther P. Jackson, the local Black high school.

We worked hard on the farm. We had chores to perform and were held accountable for getting them done with little oversight or follow-up. No one woke me up at 5:00am, and reminded me that I had six cows to milk and feed before leaving for school. Harvest season required teamwork between me, my siblings and the occasional hired hand, with much negotiating about our respective roles. For example, when it was time to harvest the hay, we had a vigorous debate about who would drive the truck. We would all argue our position, but once the decision was made, we fully committed to getting the job done right. Everyone understood what needed to be done and when. With different planting, growing and harvesting seasons and the unpredictability of the weather, a delay could result in the loss of an entire year's production, and that would have been costly. Whether it was picking tobacco, cutting corn, harvesting wheat or attending to the 3,500 chickens and 2,500 turkeys, we all knew that anything less than perfect execution could have disastrous results. Can you imagine what would happen if you accidentally left the doors to the chicken house open and 3,500 chickens escaped? We were collaborating, gathering diverse opinions and practicing teamwork without the assistance of a consultant or attending a single workshop on how effective teams operate. Imagine that! Working on the farm had taught us cooperation was better than division, that two heads are better than one, that everybody's opinion should be respected and that the good of the group, the family, trumps the interest of any one group member.

While my parents insisted we all work hard, they also knew the benefits of rewards and recognitions. Therefore, each one of us was given at least one chore where we could earn money, an allowance, of sorts. Mine was the dairy operation. I had been milking cows since I was six, but at ten I was taught how to drive the pick-up truck and given the added responsibilities of processing the milk into ten gallon cans, placing the cans in a big cooler, removing the prior day's milk, loading it onto the pickup and driving five miles to meet the milk truck from A &P. For this, I earned a certain percentage of the income from the milk sales. In a few years I had saved enough money to open my first bank account. It was relatively easy to save money, because where we lived there was little a ten-year old could buy. Additionally, it was time for me to start saving for my education; house rules.

One of my other rewards for hard work and good grades was going with my stepfather to Farmville to sell our tobacco. This was a major adventure and one of the highlights of the year. We would separate the tobacco into different grades based on the quality of the leaf, bind similar grades together and load them on the pickup. Then we would drive twenty-five miles to the tobacco warehouses in Farmville where we unloaded our tobacco and put it in huge baskets placed in long lines down the floor of the warehouse. Each farmer received a batch number. The buyers and the auctioneer would arrive to inspect the leaf. This was the moment of truth. The auctioneer walked the aisles getting bids on each batch. After the sale we collected our money and went home. We did this three or four times a year. Some of the trips were during the Christmas holidays, so occasionally we would do a little shopping before heading home. If it was a good year, we all shared in the proceeds from tobacco sales, so everyone at home was anxious for our return. Usually, it was good news. Tobacco was our biggest cash crop, so everyone was involved with its production and processing and shared in the income.

I don't recall ever having a strategic or operational plan, at least one that was written down or the result of a formal planning session. However, there is no doubt, without the formality, we had all of the elements of both plans. In hindsight, the planning and execution necessary to run such a diverse operation, with a rookie staff, had to be rather sophisticated. We had a vision, a mission, very specific objectives, metrics to measure outcomes, assigned responsibilities, rewards and recognition for good performance.

We just didn't call it that. Fortunately, years later when I found myself In a corporate environment, where the process was more formal, the basics of what we did on the farm, stayed with me and I was able to apply the labels and use the same process that had been so successful in my youth.

    Concepts that others had to learn were second nature to me. I didn't have to learn to trust my fellow colleagues; it was the only way I knew how to relate. I didn't have to learn to collaborate; it was the only way I knew how to make sure the best ideas were always on the table. Candor, for me was a given and anything less was not only unexpected, but was to be scorned and considered dishonest. Setting high standards for me and all those around me was the only way I knew how to perform, since in my world failure was never an option. Holding people accountable was not the flavor of the week, but rather how I expected all around me to deliver, recognizing that no chain is any stronger than its weakest link. Soliciting different ideas/perspectives before making a decision was the only way I knew how to make decisions, so this was natural to me. I learned how to use that advantage to achieve superior results in every assignment I received.

    Fortunately, for me and my siblings, our mother shared our father's commitment to education and the belief that it was the key to success, not only for minorities, but for everyone trying to improve their station in life. (My mother completed the seventh grade, which, at the time, was the highest grade available locally). Education and getting smarter was always a central theme in our family. We always had the latest edition of the Encyclopedia Britannica, and when asked a question, my mother's frequent response was, "Look it up". This technique not only gave us the information we needed, but also began to teach us the value of research and how to conduct it. For current events, we subscribed to Life magazine. My mother believed that information was power and she instilled that belief in all of us.

    Despite the demands of the farm, we were all expected to excel in school. Any grade lower than a B on a report card, would result in the severest of punishments from Miss Rena, and we all wanted to avoid that at all cost. One of my mother's most amazing accomplishments, in my opinion, was that of eight children, all attended college, four graduated, and two left early, but finished nursing school. My third sister dropped out, married a career soldier and traveled the world for 20 plus years. Three of my sisters followed in our father's footsteps and became teachers, dedicating more than 30 years each to various public school systems in Virginia. I have always admired my sisters, for to me, nothing is more important than teaching our children. My hope is still that one day our society will recognize this and start treating teachers with respect and reward them as they deserve.

When I was six my formal education started in the Pine Grove Elementary School, a segregated, two-room school that was home to about 25 students in grades one through six. Our teacher was Mrs. Betty Lou Scales. For the first three years I had to walk three miles each way to school. Surprisingly, I don't recall any of us seeing this as a hardship. Rather, we enjoyed the walks because it gave us time to spend with our friends, but I do recall us being rather happy when we got to ride the bus to school. There's only so much fun you can stand. My years at Pine Grove are pretty much a blur. However, I remember that all grades were exposed to the same material and Mrs. Scales would often encourage fourth graders to do sixth-grade work. In other words, we could work at whatever level our capabilities allowed. I always thought this was a good way to learn.

In addition to school, our education continued at home. We had Scrabble, Monopoly, chess and checkers, both traditional and Chinese. We would spend hours late in the evening playing games. One advantage of a large family is that you always have playmates. My mother loved poetry and would often read to us. One of her favorite poems was: The House by the Side of the Road by Sam Walter Foss.

The House by the Side of the Road

There are hermit
souls that live withdrawn

In the peace of their self-content;
There are souls, like stars, that dwell apart,
In a fellowless firmament;
There are pioneer souls that blaze their paths
Where highways never ran:
But let me live by the side of the road
And be a friend to man.

Let me live in a house
by the side of the road,
Where the race of men go by;
The men who are good and the men who are bad,
As good and as bad as I.
I would not sit in the scorner's seat,
Or hurl the cynic's ban;
Let me live in the house by the side of the road
And be a friend to man.

I see from my house
by the side of the road,
By the side of the highway of life,
The men who press with ardor of hope,
The men who are faint with the strife.
But I turn not away from their smiles nor their tears,
Both parts of an infinite plan,
Let me live in my house by the side of the road
And be a friend to man

I know there are brook-gladdened
meadows ahead
And mountains of wearisome height;
That the road passes on through the long afternoon
and stretches away to the night.
But still I rejoice when the travelers rejoice.
And weep with the strangers that moan.
Nor live in my house by the side of the road
Like a man who dwells alone.

Let me live in my
house by the side of the road
Where the race of men go by-
They are good, they are bad, they are weak,
they are strong.
Wise, foolish-so am I
Then why should I sit in the scorner's seat
Or hurl the cynic's ban?
Let me live in the house by the side of the road
And be a friend to man.

It is no wonder this was my mother's favorite poem since it reflects a lot of her personal beliefs. She could be often heard reciting it as she worked away on the farm.

As a child, I had a very good memory, and upon discovering this, my mother required me to learn several poems and recite them at church and local talent events. I learned to be comfortable speaking in public, and it is one of the most valuable assets I would take from my childhood. Public speaking is one of the most treasured skills anyone can have and the development of my ability started at an early age. Over the years I honed these skills and became a very effective public speaker.

One of my favorite poem was; "It Couldn't Be Done" by Edgar Albert Guest. Ironic!

It Couldn't Be Done

Somebody said that it couldn't be done
But he with a chuckle replied
That maybe it couldn't, but he would be one
Who wouldn't say so 'til he'd tried.
So he buckled right in with the trace of a grin
On his face. If he worried he hid it.

He started to sing as he tackled the thing
That couldn't be done, and he did it!

Somebody scoffed: Oh, you'll never do that;
At least no one ever has done it;
But he took off his coat and he took off his hat
And the first thing we knew he'd begun it.
With a lift of his chin and a bit of a grin,
Without any doubt or quiddit,
He started to sing as he tackled the thing
That couldn't be done, and he did it.

There are thousands to tell you it cannot be done,
There are thousands to prophesy failure,
There are thousands to point out to you one by one,
The dangers that wait to assail you.
But just buckle in with a bit of a grin,
Just take off your coat and go to it;
Just start in to sing as you tackle the thing
That cannot be done, and you'll do it.

As a youngster I would recite these and several other poems many times at a variety of events. I became so good at it that people invited me to perform on their programs, much to the delight of my family.

When I entered the seventh grade, I transferred to Luther P. Jackson High School, the Black high school for Cumberland County. My oldest sister, Cassandra, taught math there, so I entered with some degree of status. Not one to squander resources, I took full advantage, and as a seventh grader was very outspoken on a variety of issues. By this time, I had started to become self-confident, forming my own opinions about things. In high school I often challenged the status quo. While we were fortunate to have some very good, well-educated teachers, they were not quite ready for questioning students. I was always ready to push the edges of the envelope, and as such, was frequently asked to leave class. I would take refuge in the library where a family friend was the librarian. Whenever I arrived, she would query me on the issue that got me ejected from class. Frequently she would point me to a reference and the two of us would explore the topic. Even when she knew the answer to my question she guided me through the process of learning it for myself. This resulted in fortifying my position, or blowing holes in it. In the latter case, I was required to apologize to the teacher.

Despite knowing that my mother would not be pleased and that I risked punishment, I continued my classroom battles. I would get a pretty good tongue lashing, but nothing more. In hindsight her discipline was not as harsh as it might have been. I think at some level she didn't want to discourage me from speaking out and vigorously representing my point of view, recognizing that this would serve me well in the future.

However, she was very unhappy when I got kicked out of Vacation Bible School for questioning the meaning of a passage from the Bible. The passage was "Every man is saved by his own belief". I took the position that if that were literally true, atheists, who truly didn't believe, would be saved. Following a rather intense debate, the instructor asked me to leave. After a severe reprimand and my less than heartfelt apology, my mother got me reinstated. Vacation Bible School was never the same after that experience and I merely tolerated it.

During this time, I also developed an affinity for great quotes. My philosophy was that if something had already been stated in an eloquent fashion, I shouldn't try to improve on it. I acquired a copy of Barlett's Familiar Quotations, which I still have on my desk. Over the years, I acquired several other books of quotations and throughout my career I used them frequently.

My mother had a younger brother, James, a very successful entrepreneur who lived in Chicago, and we considered him to be the intellectual of the family. I looked forward to his frequent visits; he was the only other person I knew who would argue with me for hours on any subject. It was not uncommon for us to stay up all night and discuss the current hot topic. When Uncle James came to visit, it was always an opportunity for me to test and hone my debate skills, important in my future learning. I also knew that

I had to make sure my information was correct and current because I knew he would challenge and exploit any weakness in my positions. A good, on-point quote was always effective in these discussions.

When I was fourteen, my willingness to speak up was really put to the test. While helping my stepfather cut fire wood with a huge circular saw powered by a tractor, my hand slipped off a log, into the saw. My right arm was cut, to the bone, at the elbow. My parents rushed me to the local doctor, who upon examination, announced that my arm was so badly damaged, that the only thing they could do was amputate. I said to the doctor, "I'm fourteen years old and can't see myself going through life with one arm, so there must be another answer". After some discussion, he said that some new work was being done to re-attach tendons, but he was not sure of the success rate. To explore this possibility, I had to travel to Community Hospital in Farmville, where I was born, to see a specialist. The specialist was not very optimistic. He would try to save my arm, but I might lose all use of it. I said I would take my chances. After a lengthy and painful recovery, I retained the use of my arm and with the exception of some occasional discomfort, it is still fully functional. I have often wondered how different my life would have been had I not spoken up. While my parents loved me very much, and always had my best interest at heart, they were not accustomed to questioning the experts: Another lesson preparing me for my unpredictabe future.

In high school I participated in several extracurricular activities. My arm injury prevented me from playing sports, but I was active in several clubs, sang in the school choir, was a member of the 4-H club, and the New Farmers of America (NFA). It was in those organizations that I learned to compete and win. For example, in the 4-H Club, I raised and trained prized pigs to show and sell at the County Fair and planted pine seedlings to replenish forest land. In the NFA I was elected a State Officer in my senior year and participated in the state forestry judging contest, (where I had to identify a number of different tree species), and the Public Speaking Contest. I did okay in tree identification, but my real success came in Public Speaking. I won the local, state, and regional competitions and placed third in the nationals which were held in Atlanta Georgia. My many years of reciting poems in front of groups was already starting to pay off.

I graduated from Luther P. Jackson on June 10, 1966, in a class of 43 students. I was not the valedictorian, I was not even the salutatorian, but I was an Honor Student and was voted by my classmates, "The most likely to Succeed". I enjoyed high school and was an eager learner. There the lessons from the Farm, the Family and various academic sources started to jell and my life philosophies started to really take hold. My confidence was at an all-time high and I felt like the world was waiting.

Growing up watching Perry Mason on TV, I had decided that I wanted to become a lawyer, the next Clarence Darrow. Given my communication skills and my passion for debate, everyone around me thought this was an excellent choice. For years I had practiced closing arguments, cross-examining witnesses, and producing the smoking gun that would blow the case wide open. I was now ready to pursue that dream with all the vigor, excitement and anticipation one could muster. I applied to and was accepted to Hampton Institute, now Hampton University, in Hampton Virginia. While my father, oldest sister and second youngest sister had attended Virginia Union University, in Richmond, my youngest sister, graduated from Hampton. I got to visit her several times and fell in love with the school. It had an excellent academic reputation, probably the best Historically Black College in the country, although people from Howard University in Washington DC would argue to the contrary. It also had, and this is not in dispute, a gorgeous campus situated on the Hampton River, which offered spectacular views and endless recreational activities.

I left home three days after graduating from high school and moved to Richmond, Virginia, living with my second youngest sister, Joyce and her husband Earl. The Farm part of my life was over, and I was anxious to get on with the next phase. While the farm was good to us, I never once considered staying there, I knew that I was destined to do something else, and I couldn't wait to find out what that was. Mark Twain once said, **"The two most important days in one's life are the day we are born and the day we find out why"**. My "why" was still a mystery.

My plan was to get a job for the summer and make some money for school. I had watched my mother struggle to help my sisters through college, and I was determined to do it on my own. I had secured a student loan, but that was not enough. I quickly got a job working in a plant that cut and shaped steel reinforcement bars for the concrete industry. It was hard, dirty work, but I had been trained on the farm and there was nothing I couldn't handle. The pay was also very good. Things were going really well; I was enjoying my independence, making money, getting to know and like the city and finalizing plans to attend Hampton in September.

Then in August I met an Air force recruiter. At this time, the Viet Nam war was raging and we still had the draft. My college deferment was not guaranteed and the recruiter convinced me the Air Force was a safe alternative to the draft; that would allow me to have at least some control over where I was deployed. So in late August I announced to the family I would not be attending Hampton, but instead, joining the US Air Force. My sisters tried to be supportive, but could not hide their disappointment. My mother made it clear that this was the biggest mistake I could possibly make and would ruin my life forever. She also made it clear that she could not believe my father's only son would dishonor his memory by not pursuing higher education, to which he had dedicated his life. (My mother didn't always fight fair) I was not deterred. I was going to become a Fly Boy. But my mother wasn't finished. She decided to call the one person she believed had the best chance of winning an argument with me, Uncle James!

I arrived home from work one day and Uncle James was sitting in the backyard, under a tree, drinking ice tea. I was surprised to see him since his visit was unannounced. It was the first time in my life that my uncle and I did not debate a subject. He made it clear right from the start that he was not there to argue, he was there to take me to school. He reiterated my mother's sentiment, that given my father's belief in education, his only son was going to college, and that he was there to make sure that happened.

Since I have never been one to fight a losing battle, I acquiesced and agreed to attend Hampton. The next day, we packed my belongings into Uncle James' station wagon and headed to Hampton. I have often wondered what my life would have been like had my mother not cared enough to intervene and perhaps prevent me from making a huge mistake.

Because of my indecision, I arrived on campus two days late, so I missed most of freshman orientation and a lot of the other things that freshmen do, like get a campus job. So after I registered and signed in, I headed to the student placement office to get a job, since I still did not have enough money to make it on my own. Uncle James had offered financial support, but I refused. The lady in the placement office almost laughed at me and said, "Alfred, you're late and all of the jobs have been taken." I replied "but you don't understand I need a job." After several minutes of back and forth, where I insisted that a place as large as this must have a job somewhere, she admitted there was one job left, but it was reserved for a young lady. I asked why it was reserved for a girl. She said the job was for a secretary, in the women's Physical Education department, in an office located in the rear of the girls' locker room. I could tell immediately that this was going to take more persuasive skill than I had ever needed before but that job was going to be mine. I said I had taken typing in high school, and could type 50 words per minute. In addition, I grew up with six older sisters and was quite comfortable around naked females. She actually found this humorous. We bantered back and forth for several more minutes. Finally she said, "Alfred, I don't think this is going to work, but I am going to let you talk to Dr. Bell, the head of the Department. If you can convince her that it's okay, you can have the job".

Armed with the job description, I headed to Dr. Bell's office. I was always pretty good at reading people, and as soon as I walked through the door, I knew this was my lucky day. Dr. Bell was a rebel, and rebels love nothing more than upsetting the status quo! A male secretary, working in an office in the rear of the girl's locker room was sure to cause some excitement. She was a little skeptical at first, I think only because this was an opportunity she wasn't expecting that day, but quickly warmed to the idea. I kept that job for two years! I have often referred to it as the best job I ever had, for obvious reasons, but also for reasons not so obvious.

That experience gave me the foundation for relating to people, in both my professional and personal life, for the rest of my life. I learned people can be convinced of almost anything if your motives are pure and your arguments convincing and sincere. People are naturally inclined to be helpful and giving if there is an atmosphere of trust and respect. Contrary to popular belief, TRUST does not have to be earned, DISTRUST does. Dr. Bell had just met me, knew little about me, but was willing to trust me in what could have been a very delicate situation, because she had no reason to distrust me. She also saw a person in need and her natural impulse was to help, even if it required extraordinary measures. I have always believed that most, people are like Dr. Bell.

I also learned how adaptable people are. In less than two weeks the young ladies were perfectly comfortable with me being in their locker room, and would pass my door, mostly nude, and greet me like one of the girls. I have often heard in major companies that employees resist or fear change. In my experience, nothing could be further from the truth. People relish change because it is consistent with their adaptive nature, as long as the change promotes the common good, and is conducted in an environment of trust, fairness and respect.

Finally, challenging the status quo can be an awful lot of fun and produce incredible results, sometimes when you least expect it. Over the two years I had this job, my role expanded significantly. In addition to my typing duties, I became chauffeur, babysitter, tutor and equipment manager for the girls' sports teams. Two of the professors I worked for had school-age children, so I would pick them up from school, take them home, babysit until their parents arrived, and help with homework. This gave me access to a car, so I could be seen driving around campus, usually in a new Lincoln Continental. As equipment manager, I got to travel with the teams. Bus rides to the away games were always great fun. I still think this was the best job I ever had!!!

With my finances in place, it was time to focus on classes. I had decided to major in Political Science, because I was preparing to become the next Clarence Darrow. Also, my aptitude for the applied sciences was near zero. I had discovered years earlier that I was definitely "right brained". My oldest sister and my youngest were mathematicians, so that gene was completely depleted by the time I was born. The head of the Math Department at Hampton once told me he did not believe I was my sister's brother because she was so good and I so bad. That was fine with me since lawyering was my chosen profession and lawyers didn't have to be experts in math. So I chose my classes carefully, favoring history, government and civic courses. Unfortunately, math, biology and a foreign language were required subjects for all majors. I slid through biology okay, but math was a real struggle, and I was lucky to escape with a D. French was my chosen foreign language and I failed, twice. (I decided to postpone it until the bitter end which resulted in having to take six hours of French, in summer school, following my senior year).

Social Studies proved to be a wise choice for me. I found in college what I had been searching for throughout high school: teachers that loved debating as much as I did. I thoroughly enjoyed these classes and excelled in class participation, a big part of our grade. I was also a pretty good writer, and I rarely got less than an A on my papers. I didn't sweat the other stuff, math, biology and French, because I had already started to learn that sweating the small stuff was a bad idea, and was to be avoided at all cost. And my mother was far enough away that I didn't have to be concerned about the long arm of the law from a disciplinary standpoint. Things were going well for me and I was enjoying every minute.

In the 60s there was a lot more happening on college campuses than learning. This was a magical, albeit tumultuous, time in our history when the world order was being reset and the Baby Boomer generation was coming into its own. We saw our mission as righting the wrongs we had inherited. From the Viet Nam war, to civil rights, to establishment policies we deemed no longer appropriate, we set out to put in motion a revolution that would ultimately define a generation.

I participated in several civil rights demonstrations, although I was not a fan of Dr. King's non-violent approach. I understood his rationale, had nothing but admiration for Dr. King, but clearly understood that my temperament would not allow me to turn the other cheek when attacked or threatened. I was starting to realize the value of knowing your limitations, and being comfortable with them.

The war protests were as intense as the civil rights movement. We were losing thousands of American soldiers, some of them our relatives, classmates and friends, in a war effort that very few understood and even fewer supported. The one thing I regretted about these protests is they were often confused with protests against our men and women in uniform. That was never the case. We had nothing but the utmost respect and admiration for these young men and women who fought and died for their country.

While all of this was going on, there were also on-campus establishment rules and regulations to challenge. The first was the girls' curfew. During my freshman year, freshman girls had to be locked in their dorm rooms by 11:00pm, even on weekends. We decided to stage a protest on the waterfront. One Friday evening, all freshman girls and boys took their mattresses and headed for the water. We vowed to sleep outside on the waterfront until the policy was changed. It was changed rather quickly.

Emboldened by our success with the curfew, we decided to attack the school's ROTC policy. At Hampton, as well as several other southern schools, ROTC was required for all boys for their freshman and sophomore years. While we strongly supported ROTC, we felt that it should be an elective. So one Monday, which was our drill day, we cadets dumped our uniforms in the middle of the drill field. This got intense very quickly when the administration decided that, rather than try to deal with hundreds of disgruntled cadets, it would call in the US Army.

Since ROTC was run by the Army, this was a rather obvious call that we, the protesters, had overlooked. Hampton is located in Tidewater Virginia, home to several military bases. Within minutes of the call from campus a half-dozen military helicopters circled the drill field. Voices boomed from loudspeakers warning us we were in violation of several military regulations and subject to arrest and court marital. We stood our ground, thinking that despite the show of force, they would never fire on a group of unarmed students, particularly since the local media were now on the scene. Fortunately, we were right and the demonstration ended peacefully. Negotiations ensued, and the following year, ROTC was an elective.

Our next initiative was the elimination of Greek Organizations on campus, both sororities and fraternities. For some reason, and now I can't remember why, we decided these organizations were brutal, and contrary to the social order. We organized groups of freshmen to disrupt Hell Week. Our tactic was to interrupt the harassment of new pledges. We won that year, but had no sustainable effort. Well, you can't win them all. Wisely, we moved on to more important issues.

My last defining moment at Hampton was a tragic one. For Memorial Day 1968, I came to Richmond, as I often did, to visit my family. I was staying with Joyce, my second youngest sister. Lottie, my third youngest sister, was married to a wonderful guy, named Louis Kersey. Louis was a veteran of Viet Nam, a true friend and brother, and completely dedicated to the well-being of his family. Lottie had two children from a previous marriage and she and Louis had one son. I arrived in Richmond on Thursday and was hanging out in the backyard with my brother-in-law, Earl and several of his friends. Louis was working that day, but had heard I was in town. On his lunch hour, he dropped by to say hello and make plans for the weekend. After a short visit, he left to return to work. Just minutes after he left, we heard a loud crash. We rushed up the street to see two badly mangled vehicles. A drunk driver had run a stop sign and hit Louis head on, killing him. The other driver received only minor injuries. We were devastated. In those short moments I was confronted with one of the harshest lessons life can serve up. That was the fragility and uncertainly we all face, but seldom acknowledge. That living for the day, the moment is something we all should strive for, but seldom accomplish. For life is not a destination, but a journey and every minute, every second, could be our last. I can't say that I completely embraced this idea, but it did give me a whole new outlook on life and I have always attempted to enjoy the moment and not put off for tomorrow things that should be done today.

I enjoyed my first two years of college and truly believe I got the most out of the experience. To this day, I have a closer affinity to Hampton than Virginia Union, from where I actually graduated, mainly because of the total college experience I had there. At Virginia Union my objectives were totally different, but as you will see later, completely fulfilled my goals, and was, in large part, responsible for me landing in my unanticipated career.

I knew I needed a college degree to get into law school. For some reason, I had decided that I should own a car, but I couldn't afford to buy one and stay at Hampton. However, I could transfer to Virginia Union, live with one of my sisters, work in a real part-time job, buy a car and get my degree. It was difficult to leave the ladies, but in September 1968 I transferred to Virginia Union University.

With the help of a brother-in-law, I got a part-time job at M & B Headwear, at the time the largest manufacturer of military headwear in the country. My job was to perform menial tasks around the factory, such as sweeping the floor, taking out trash and unloading material. But, I was not a menial task kind of guy. It didn't take long before I learned that the highest paid technical position, outside of management, was that of Cutter. In the manufacture of hats, we would spread 50 to 100 layers of fabric on long tables with a pattern sheet for various style hats on top. The cutter cut the fabric in the precise shape of the pattern, so the pieces could be sewn together by the hundreds of ladies at the sewing machines. Accuracy was critical; a bad cut could result in the loss of thousands of dollars.

After about a month, I approached the factory manager and informed him I wanted to be a Cutter. Even though good cutters were in short supply, he laughed and said I had neither the experience nor the commitment for him to waste time training me.

After all, I was a part-time employee, destined to leave as soon as I completed school. I couldn't argue with his logic, but did disagree with his assessment of the investment in my training. A couple of weeks later, I approached him again, and shared my feelings. I told him I had been watching the Cutters and felt I could do the job with no further training. After a lengthy discussion/debate, he agreed to give me a test. I passed with flying colors. He was amazed, but from that day forward, I was a Cutter.

Not only did this give me a significant increase in my income, it allowed me to work flexible hours. I could come to work at 5:00am and work until 10:00am before class, or I could work at night until whatever time I wanted. So I got a raise and increased hours that allowed me to easily afford a car. I brought a 1966 Chevelle Super Sport 396, Cinnamon with Black interior. I loved that car. I was now, not only mobile, but mobile in style. This was clearly another example of my Dr. Bell experience and reinforced those learning's. I would continue to work at M & B until I graduated in 1970.

Because I lived off campus, my stay at Virginia Union was totally different than at Hampton. My only campus activity was attending class. Union didn't have a Political Science Major, so I had to change my major to History and Government, which was very similar and offered the same type classes. I also decided to take some courses in Sociology. My first semester was very uneventful. My job was going well, I was enjoying my new car and I thought all was right with the world.

That would all change in January 1969. I turned 21 years old on January 12, 1969. My sisters and several friends had planned a surprise birthday party. The party was a blast! Then on January 13th, my sisters informed me I had received a letter the day before that they did not give me, because they didn't want to spoil the celebration. They handed me the letter. You guessed it, Greetings from Uncle Sam. I was momentarily devastated, but quickly recovered. With Viet Nam in full bloom, there was no way I could see myself being drafted into the Army. I did some quick research and discovered that transferring to Virginia Union and changing my Major, had caused my average semester hours to fall below the requirement for keeping my college deferment. I had made a huge mistake by not considering all of the consequences of my decision, a painful lesson learned, but one I would never forget.

I had few options, so deciding what to do was relatively easy. Moving to Canada, as a lot of people did during this time, was not for me, because I could no more see myself as a fugitive for the rest of my life as I could see myself a soldier. Somehow, I needed to convince Uncle Sam to change his mind.

Cumberland is a small community, where everybody knows everybody, so I had known the head of the Selective Service all my life. I called her and asked for her assistance. She informed me I had been drafted and, as much as she wished she could, there was nothing she or anybody else could do. I insisted there had to be some solution. After a pretty lengthy discussion, she said she knew the head of the state Selective Service, and would try to get him to meet with me, but that would be an unusual request, and she didn't think there was anything he could do anyway. I said we should try. Two days later, she called me back and said the Major would meet with me. I had an appointment at 10:00am the following Wednesday, in his office in Richmond, Virginia.

I arrived for my appointment at 9:30am. Promptly at 10:00am, I was ushered into the major's office. I'm not sure what I was expecting, but the major was not what I had imagined. He was very pleasant, very polite, almost apologetic and except for the uniform, reminded me more of a college professor than a soldier. Since he already knew why I was there, our initial discussions centered around why I didn't want to go into the Army. I tried to be as tactful as possible. After all, I was talking to a soldier at the same time, conveying a strong conviction to my arguments. He had what seemed like, an endless number of questions. As the morning progressed, we covered every topic under the sun, from my childhood, my family, my beliefs and a lot about what I wanted to be when I grew up. Two hours passed and the major offered to take me to lunch, and of course, I accepted. Our conversation continued. We returned to his office and talked for probably another hour or so. I was feeling good about our session. Finally he said, "Alfred, you have been drafted into the United States Army, with a report date in two weeks. There is absolutely nothing I can do to change your orders, but I can change the date you have to report". Since I had already started the second semester at Union, he would change my report date to the middle of June, to allow me to finish the semester. He asked if this was acceptable, to which I replied, I was hoping for a more permanent solution, but would accept this in the meantime. After a warm handshake, he informed me in three days, I would receive another letter from the Selective Service, advising my orders remain the same, but my new report date would be June 15th. If I did not receive the letter, I was to call him. I thanked him, told him how much I enjoyed our time together, and said if he came up with a better solution before June 15th, I would really appreciate it. He laughed, said he wished he could, but that was not likely. He also said how much he enjoyed our discussions and wished me luck with my life and career. I left his office feeling somewhat victorious, since I had gotten a reprieve, but realizing the task ahead was going to be difficult. The Major had made it clear; there was little anybody could do to change my Orders.

In three days, I received my letter, just as the major promised, but instead of stating June 15th as my new report date, it rescinded my original date, and said I would be contacted by June 15th with a new report date. It was a little different than I expected, but didn't cause me any concern. I went on with my life with the Sword of Damocles hanging over my head. My classes were pretty much uneventful, I was still enjoying my car, and the hat business was booming. Beginning on June 11th, I checked the mailbox daily, for THE LETTER. June 15 passed and still no letter had come. Not being one to look a gift horse in the mouth, I did not call to inquire. Then July came and went; August passed without a letter. Feeling great relief, I enrolled for the first semester of my senior year.

I am absolutely convinced the major did something to make sure I didn't get a new date. If I needed any more proof my premise was correct, this was it in spades. If your motives are pure, your rationale convincing and sincere and the interaction takes place in an atmosphere of trust and mutual respect, you can convince people to do almost anything. People want to be helpful and they will take extraordinary measures to do so.

During the Viet Nam War the draft was a subject of protest, seen unfairly administered in favor of wealthier American men. On November 26, 1969 President Nixon signed an amendment to the Military Selective Service Act of 1967 that established a lottery for the draft. Under this system, each day of the year was assigned a number from 1 to 366, and randomly selected. Eligible young men born on the selected dates in the order they were drawn, were drafted. The first lottery was held on December 1, 1969. My birthday, January 12, was the 221th number drawn. Induction reached 195 for that year. I had avoided the draft forever; that is unless someone found the original notice, which I doubted, would ever happen. It is estimated that by 1972, 125,000 draft evaders were living in Canada.

In May of 1970 I had completed all of the requirements for a BA degree in Social Sciences, from Virginia Union, except the mandatory foreign language credits. I took six hours of French in summer school, somehow passed, and was done with college! My mother was relieved and delighted! So was Uncle James.

I had dated my High School sweetheart all through college, and my mother and her parents assumed we would get married upon graduation. So, sometime during the spring of 1970, our parents planned our wedding. You might say I drifted into marriage. It's not that I didn't want to marry her. It was more not knowing what I wanted, so on June 7, 1970 we were wed. She had graduated from Virginia State College, now University, with a degree in Accounting. We planned she would get a job, and I would attend law school.

The job market in the summer of 1970 was very poor and my new wife was unable to find a job. As September approached, we decided our plans might have to be adjusted. During the summer, I had received several letters from Aetna Life & Casualty Insurance Company, asking me to come in to be tested, interviewed and possibly offered a job in one of their technical positions. Aetna, at the time the largest diversified, financial institution in the world, was also a very large government contractor. The continuation of their contracts hinged on meeting the affirmative action requirements imposed by the recently passed Civil Rights Act. Since at the time, Aetna didn't have minorities or females in its technical positions, they were almost desperate to comply. My wife agreed I should pursue this opportunity and if I got the job, work for one year during which she should be able to find a job, and then I would go to law school. I called Aetna and made an appointment.

I arrived for my appointment in the Richmond office, was tested, interviewed and offered a job on the spot. I was told I made the highest score ever on their test. I questioned that since taking standardized tests was not one of my strong suits. Their offer was for a claim representative trainee with a starting salary of $7,800 per year. I would train in the Richmond office for about a year but then be subject to transfer to any one of their 60 branch offices throughout the country. I would receive a raise at the end of my training period and if transferred, the company would pay all expenses. It sounded like a really good deal, but I told them I had to discuss it with my wife and I would give them an answer in two days. This certainly would fulfill our needs, but I knew nothing about Aetna, and even less about the insurance industry, so I thought it advisable to do a little research before I jumped in. The time I spent "looking things up" at home, preparing for Uncle James' visits and the hours in the library, were about to pay off.

Aetna was founded in 1853 as a life insurance company. Its name was inspired by Mt. Etna, an active volcano located on the eastern shores of Sicily. It was currently headquartered at 151 Farmington Avenue, Hartford Ct. Over the years, it had expanded its product lines, and was now a multi-line insurer involved in all lines of insurance. It had also been involved in some of the major historical events of the time. Among others, it provided the bonding coverage for the construction of the Hoover Dam, the National Archives Building in Washington DC, several Navy aircraft carriers, and the United Nations headquarters in New York. It had provided the insurance coverage for the Manhattan Project, and the first seven astronauts. In 1944, Aetna was the first insurance company to advertise on television. Aetna had several international partnerships and employed more than 50,000 people worldwide, 15,000 working at its home office. The home office building was the largest colonial structure in the world. Aetna had a reputation of being a very conservative company, run by white males, and relatively content with its current state.

I was impressed and intrigued with this new opportunity. Until this point, my only exposure/ knowledge of insurance, was the life insurance guy coming by once a month to collect $5.00 from my mother for her life insurance premium. The breadth and depth to which insurance was involved in so many different things astounded me. Even though this was supposed to be a temporary job, I was getting excited about the opportunity to explore a whole new world. I accepted the job and started work for Aetna on August 8, 1970.

ABANDONING THE DREAM

My excitement only grew after I accepted the job with Aetna. My curiosity had been stoked by the limited research I had conducted and I was anxious to learn more about Aetna and the insurance industry. Aetna was organized into three main divisions; the Employee Benefits Division which sold life insurance, annuities, and health insurance to both companies and individuals, the International Division which sold most products in foreign countries, and the Property and Casualty Division which sold property and liability insurance to companies and individuals in the United States. I would be working in the Property and Casualty Division. The P&C Division was organized around a branch office structure. There were 60 or so branch offices, located in major cities, throughout the United States. We also had operations in Canada and Puerto Rico. Branches were supported by a massive home office structure. The branches were headed by a general manager and included all of the functions necessary to write and service the business. This included, underwriting, marketing, loss control, administration and claims, all headed by managers. The general manager position was the most coveted job in the company since branches were run pretty autonomously, as separate profit centers. These positions were reserved for the most experienced, seasoned professionals with many years of service, and a proven track record in achieving superior results. They had a dress code requiring dark suits, white shirts and dark ties. Hats were mandatory in public. New GM's had to attend charm school to insure they had all of the social graces befitting their lofty position.

Jobs within the company were identified through a class system. Exempt, technical jobs carried classes 26 through 30. Classes 31 and above represented supervisory and management positions. Each class had a specific job description and salary range. Claim representative trainees were class 26. Two other minorities were hired in claims in the Richmond office with me. We were very fortunate to be hired in this branch. Because of the high quality of life in Richmond, people rarely transferred out, so they had a very experienced staff. Several of the claims representatives had 20 plus years with the company.

The General Manager of the Richmond office, an ex-marine, austere and reserved, was a by-the-book manager. As a trainee, I seldom saw him. The manager of the claims department had 30 years in the business. Reporting to him was a superintendent and several supervisors responsible for units that handled different type claims: i.e. homeowners, auto liability, auto physical damage, workers compensation and general liability, including products. Assignments were made based on the experience level of the claims rep. Trainees handled the smaller, less complicated files with smaller payouts, where they learned the basic investigative techniques necessary for all claims.

In addition to size and complexity, there were two contractual categories for claims; First Party and Third Party. First-party claims, (those people who paid premiums and were policy holders) involved losses such as those from house fires, thefts, and claims for damage to an automobile. Third-party claims were losses our policyholders may be liable for to another person, because of the policyholder's negligence; i.e. failure to stop at a stop sign and causing damage to another vehicle.

I was surprised to learn that law played a major role in claims handling. Investigation, contract interpretation, liability assessment and the negotiation of settlements involved legal principles and often attorneys handled third-party claims. While Aetna's policy was to settle all claims in a fair and equitable way, evaluating losses was always a challenge. I discovered early on otherwise law abiding citizens find it perfectly ok to cheat by inflating claim values. This was right down my alley and I found myself getting quite a legal education, without going to law school. Good claims handling also required a lot of research. In addition to the legal principles involved, I had to locate witnesses, establish the value of injuries, disabilities, pain and suffering and all manner of property items. I soon realized claim handling was very much an art and not a science. Being right-brained, and a skilled researcher, I was instantly comfortable with the claim handling process.

Shortly after I began work, the home office support team for newly hired minorities arrived in Richmond to teach us, (four others and me) how to act, and to explain the process of **assimilation.** Affirmative Action would provide a significant amount of job security, if we complied with their instructions. I had a beard at the time, and they strongly suggested I shave. This was more than I could take. After all, I had been taught my success and happiness would result from my intelligence, character, confidence and hard work. I challenged the team leader, and said I thought they were mistaken, that affirmative action, as I understood it, was to provide us the opportunity to get into the system, and prove we belonged. Assimilation was a process that made me uncomfortable, since it suggests I give up my own identity/perspective, which I considered one of my greatest assets. While conformity to certain company protocols should certainly be expected, assimilation went too far. As for my beard, while there was no one else in the Richmond office with one, it was not against the company's dress code. A huge argument broke out! After what seemed like much too long, I walked out of the meeting and never attended another one.

I was expecting to get some kind of reprimand but nothing happened. A few weeks later, the claim manager, stopped me in the hallway and said "Al, what would you say if I asked you to shave your beard"? I replied, " I am so sure you would never ask me, I haven't given it any thought." He continued on his way, as did I. Nothing was ever said about my beard again, and I kept it for the next fifteen years. Being in unfamiliar territory, didn't mean I was going to be intimidated. My mother had prepared me for that.

I can't say the environment in the Richmond office was warm and cuddly, but it wasn't openly hostile either. When it came to training, most of the people were very generous with their time and knowledge. Aetna stressed training and in the first six months I took courses in several different aspects of insurance and attended a six-week course in Hartford CT. Seeing the home office for the first time was breathtaking. Imagine 15,000 people under one roof. It had the largest fitness center and cafeteria I had ever seen. It had stores, gift shops and a bowling alley. The classes were intense, nothing like college, since they were very focused on what Aetna wanted you to learn. Debates were not a part of the agenda. My mind was like a sponge and I soaked up everything. I was determined to prove I belonged.

The course started with the basics. Insurance is a risk management tool and was first practiced by three Chinese merchants who agreed to put one-third of their cargo on each other's boat, so if one boat sunk, no one would lose everything. From that simple concept, today's huge insurance industry emerged. Insurance, today, is about the law of large numbers. The larger a group of homogeneous units of cars, boats, people or homes, the more predictable the loss experience of the group becomes. With the use of actuarial science, insurance companies predict the losses a small number of the group will have and spread that cost over the entire group with the rates they charge each policyholder.

Insurance is the financial underpinning that allows the world economy to operate. Without insurance, nothing or no one could operate because the risk would be too great. Your bank would not give you a mortgage without homeowners insurance, because you couldn't afford to replace the home if it was destroyed. Banks would not make car loans for the same reason. The place where you work would shut down because the owner could not afford to pay the medical cost of injured workers without workers' compensation insurance. Insurance companies provide the peace of mind that allows people and businesses to operate without the fear of a catastrophic occurrence destroying their financial security.

The Property and Casualty Division of Aetna is further divided into the Personal Lines Division and the Commercial Lines Division. Personal lines, handles property and liability coverage for individuals and Commercial Lines handles property, liability and workers' compensation for businesses. Aetna distributes its products through independent agents and brokers, independent businesses that represent a number of different companies.

Insurance companies are organized into four departments: underwriting, claims, loss control and marketing. The underwriting department is responsible for the selection and pricing of accounts. The loss control department serves two functions. It inspects commercial accounts for quality, including safety standards for job sites, factories and other premises, and provides this information to the underwriting department to aid in the selection process. They also make recommendations to policy holders on how to improve their operation. The marketing department manages the company's relationship with the agents and brokers. This includes negotiating commission levels, promoting new products, appointing new agents and working with underwriters to acquire and retain accounts. The claim department adjusts losses.

We also learned the fundamentals of claims handling; investigative techniques, file documentation requirements, how to interview witnesses and the various means of settlement negotiations. The importance of regulatory compliance was stressed. Each state has similar but individual regulations governing the claims resolution process and compliance is strictly enforced.

We spent a considerable amount of time discussing contracts in general and insurance contracts in particular. All of the obligations of the company on behalf of our policy holders are contained in the insurance policy, so it is imperative claims reps understand what's covered.

I found all of this fascinating and eye opening. Insurance is regarded by some as a necessary evil, something I have to buy because the state or the bank says so. As a result, the industry has never attained the level of respect it deserves. That's unfortunate.

The next several months were pretty uneventful. I was getting larger and larger claims to handle, and getting more comfortable with the process. I was learning a lot from my colleagues, whose generosity continued. My wife had gotten a job and things were going really well. As the summer of 1971 approached, I had a decision to make. I was supposed to enroll in law school. I decided I was enjoying the insurance business so much I was going to work another year.

By 1972, I was smitten. I had learned a lot about the technical aspects of insurance and also gotten to observe the role of management. I knew I wanted to be a manager, a leader. Clarence Darrow was becoming a distant memory. The thought of having to get a group of people to do things had unlimited possibilities and played directly into my beliefs. I was convinced I could become one of the company's greatest leaders. I had found my **"WHY"**. I knew, however, I had a lot to learn.

I had learned a great deal about claim handling and insurance in general. However, I knew little about management leadership styles. Aetna had an extensive leadership training program, but it was reserved for much more senior people than I was at the time. So I returned to the library. My early training in research and gathering information was again paying off.

In the 1960's, a psychologist, Douglas McGrego, of MIT put forth two contrasting theories of human motivation and leadership styles, Theory X and Theory Y. The debate over which was the more effective approach continued well into the 1970s. Theory X assumed employees were unmotivated and saw work as a necessity, thus requiring an authoritarian leadership style that directed what had to be done and how. Theory Y assumed employees are self-motivated, enjoy work, happily accept the responsibilities for getting things done, and require little direction, suggesting a highly participative leadership style.

Generally speaking, American Companies were seen as Theory X and Japanese companies as Theory Y. Managers/leaders in American companies typically came from the ranks of the best technicians in a given department. Therefore, when decisions had to be made, the head technician/manager would make the decision with little or no input from employees. On the other hand, Japanese companies believed the best leaders were those with a broad general knowledge of the company's operations. Employees were self-motivated, enjoyed work, accepted responsibility and did not have to be told what to do and how. Decisions involved employees from all levels of the organization. One of the comparisons at the time claimed American companies were quick to make decisions, but execution suffered because of the lack of buy-in from employees. Japanese companies took a long time to make decisions, but execution was flawless. I was definitely in the Theory Y camp. It almost sounded like my parents, back on the farm, had studied McGrego's work. Since I knew they hadn't, this gave the findings even more credibility.

I read the book on Theory Y from cover to cover. In fact, I studied it. I also read everything I could find on leadership. In addition, there was always ample discussion within the office, usually dealing with the ineptness of our current leaders. I spent a lot of time listening and learning what leaders should **NOT** do. After all, these were the people responsible for the execution of the leader's plans, and I felt knew better than anyone what was necessary to accomplish the objectives.

I had made the decision to make leadership at Aetna my new career and determined the type of leader I wanted to be. Now it was time to put in place just how I was going to do that. This was going to be a life/career long journey, and I wanted to get the most out of it. Up until now, this had been mostly exploratory. So using all the information I had acquired from the farm, my family, high school, Hampton, working with the ladies, Virginia Union, M & B Headwear, and my time at Aetna, I constructed my approach. I developed what I called the **Five P's For Achieving Success.** They are: 1. **PLANNING**, 2. **PREPARATION**, 3. **PROACTIVITY**, 4. **PASSION**, and 5. **PERFORMANCE**

PLANNING – Antoine de Saint – Exupery, author of The Little Prince once said, **"A goal without a Plan is just a wish".** A properly constructed plan provides a roadmap for you to achieve your goals/objectives and provides the context and framework for the decisions that you have to make along the way. It should be a working document that reflects the dynamic environment you work in. No one can predict the future with any degree of accuracy so your plan has to be flexible enough to adapt to unforeseen events and keep you on track to achieve your mission. It should contain specific, measurable, time-bound objectives that are tracked frequently. Seek input from people you think can be helpful. Try to get different perspectives so you can pick the best options.

Critical Planning Steps:

1. **Vision:** You should be able to articulate your personal vision or that of your organization in a few simple words. I like to describe it as "what you want to be when you grow up". The trick here is to distinguish between what you want to be from what you want to accomplish, which will be your mission. For example, my vision was: **"to become one of the best leaders Aetna ever had"**. Put another way, when I grew up, I wanted to be a great leader. In his book "The Seven Habits of Highly Effective People", Steven Covey calls this, "Beginning With, The End In Mind."

2. **Mission:** This defines what you want to accomplish. I wanted to have an exciting career, provide a comfortable living for my family, enjoy my work, and be the highest ranking minority in Aetna's history, when I retired. You will need milestones to continually measure your progress. If there are quantifiable parts of your mission, you should include that.

3. **Gap Analysis:** A critical step. Here you need to assess everything it will take for you to achieve your vision and mission and compare those to what you have. In my case, I wanted to be a great leader, have an exciting career, make a comfortable living and be the highest ranking minority in

Aetna's history. What did I need to make that happen? What was the skill set of a great leader and how does that compare with my current skill set? What mentors will I need to help keep my progress on track? How will I form those relationships and when? What political skills will I need to navigate the corporate environment and where will I get them? What do I need to create the strong track record of performance necessary to keep my career moving forward? Etc., etc. etc. This will be a long list. This will be the basis for all of your action steps over the life of your career. Along with the objectives that fall out of it, this is the most dynamic part of your plan. As you progress, you should always be looking for better ways to help you close a gap. You will also discover new gaps.

4. **Objectives/Goals:** Here you want to identify specific things you are going to do to close the Gaps from the above analysis. They should be measurable with expected completion dates. The action steps you identify here will become your day-to-day To Do List.

If you follow the above steps, you will have a realistic chance of turning your **WISHES** into **REALITY**.

PREPARATION – Abraham Lincoln once said; **"Give me six hours to chop down a tree, and I'll spend four sharpening the axe".** Once you have identified what you need to do to achieve your goals, you need to analyze your work environment and get out in front of the preparation. You need to anticipate what's coming and be ready to take advantage of all opportunities. You also need to position yourself to create opportunities by proposing new processes or products that will enhance the performance of your work unit. Make sure you cover all of the bases. If networking is critical to your success, start identifying the people you need to know and plan how you're going to form a relationship with them. Seek out people who are doing what you want to do and learn from them. Don't ignore the benefits of learning what not to do. This can sometimes be as beneficial as the reverse. Finally, embrace the idea that preparation is a career long-journey. The day you stop preparing is the day you have hit a plateau.

PROACTIVITY – Steven Covey said: **"People who end up with the good jobs are the proactive ones who are solutions to problems, not problems themselves, who seize the initiative to do whatever is necessary, consistent with correct principles, to get the job done"**. Be bold; be assertive. Several surveys have found one-third of the people who lost their jobs did so, not because they were doing a bad job, but because no one knew what kind of job they were doing. Be tactful, but persistent. Make sure people know what your plans are and how they can help. Don't be afraid to ask for the promotion you believe you have earned. Volunteer for difficult assignments. Develop a reputation as someone who can be counted on to get the job done right. In your approach, remember, as Grace Murray Hopper said, **"It is better to beg forgiveness than ask permission"**.

PASSION – Ralph Waldo Emerson said: **"Enthusiasm is one of the most powerful engines of success. When you do a thing, do it with all your might. Put your whole soul into it. Stamp it with your own personality. Be active, be energetic and faithful, and you will accomplish your objective. Nothing great was ever achieved without enthusiasm"**. You have to love what you do to devote the time and energy necessary to succeed. Success is a 24/7 endeavor. You won't be able to sustain that level of commitment unless you absolutely love what you're doing. Unless you suit up to play at your maximum capacity every day, you won't blow away the competition. E. M. Forster said: **"One person with passion is better than forty people merely interested"**. You always want to be that one person.

PERFORMANCE – John Eliot said: **"Great performers require a measure of confidence that would strike many as absurd, unfounded, and downright irrational. They believe in themselves utterly without question, even when everyone else is questioning how good (or sane) they are"**. Ask for the tough assignments, and then hit a home run. To out-shine your competitors, you have to outperform them. Never leave your future opportunities to chance. Out-performing the competition will always insure ever increasing opportunities to showcase your talent and enhance your value to the organization.

I had decided I wanted to be a great leader, the kind of leader I wanted to be, and developed a process to take me there. My excitement was at an all-time high. In early 1973 I got my first chance to make my next career move. One of the most coveted claim representative positions was outside claims rep. This position handled the tougher cases that required a lot of investigation, and came with a company car. We were adding one such position in Richmond and human resources was advertising for an experienced claim rep to fill it. The day after I discovered this, I met my manager in the hallway, and told him I had heard about this, and I wanted to be considered for the job. He asked if I thought I had enough experience to handle it and I said, absolutely. I pointed out to him that my files had received high marks from my supervisor on the quality of the investigations, loss evaluations and settlement negotiations, and I had gotten excellent results on several large claims, including two fatalities. He stated the position called for more years of experience than I had. I told him I thought past performance and ability should be the criteria, rather than seniority, and promised him he would not be disappointed if he gave me the job .The following week I got the job. I was elated!

During this time a lot of my social life revolved around my brother-in-law and his friends. These friends were involved in two activities, boating and playing stud poker. We would fish on the Rappahannock River and I developed a great love for the water, which my wife shared with me. I also developed a love for poker, which she did not.

One of my new friends ran a regular weekend high stakes poker game, with a $500 buy-in and maximum bets of $50. There was no training program to teach you how to play; you had to learn by doing. This proved to be a very expensive lesson for me and for about a 12 month period, I lost most of the money I earned. Fortunately, my wife paid the rent. Seeing I was on a destructive path, she asked my sisters to intervene, so a family summit was convened. As a result, I promised I would control my gambling. I knew it would be difficult to stop completely because I really enjoyed the action.

I was reasonably successful in controlling my gambling, but that twelve months had destroyed the little credit I had and I was two months behind in my student loan, and car payments. I was sitting at my desk one day when a friend called to tell me about a boat a local boat builder was trying to sell. He had built two prototypes of a speed boat he hoped to manufacture, but had run into some financial difficulties and was selling both boats. One was a twenty one foot, sleek bullet, apricot and white, with a big block engine and jet propulsion. Jet propulsion was relatively new at the time. The boat was at my friend's garage and he suggested I rush over to see it. So I jumped in my company car and headed for the garage. It was love at first sight. The boat was gorgeous, and fast, with a top speed of sixty-five miles per hour. The price tag was $5,000, and would be sold to the first person who came up with the money.

I left the garage and headed for the bank that had my delinquent car loan. I asked for the manager of the loan department. The receptionist asked if I wanted to speak to a loan officer, and I politely said no, I needed to speak to the manager. After a short wait, I was ushered into his office. I introduced myself, told him I was a customer and needed a $5,000 loan to buy a boat. He informed me the bank didn't make boat loans and the only option would be an unsecured personal loan. He had requested my records and after a short review advised me I did not qualify for a loan. I impressed upon him how much I wanted this boat, that I had a good, well-paying job, was in the process of fixing my behavior and if he approved the loan, he had my promise I would repay it in full and on time. He was not swayed. Then I told him I understood his reluctance, but assured him of my honesty, and I would never make a promise that I wouldn't keep. He agreed to take my request to the loan committee which was meeting in two days. I said, that won't work because I need the money by 5:00 this evening or the boat will be sold to someone else. He chuckled. I got up to leave and told him I knew he could approve the loan, and how much I would appreciate him doing everything he could to make it happen. I left before he could answer, because I didn't want to give him the chance to say no.

At 4:30 I got a call from the manager telling me I could stop by the bank and pick up a $5,000 cashier's check. I rushed right over, thanked the manager for his efforts, signed the paper work, reiterated my promise, picked up the check and headed to get my boat. Frankly, I couldn't believe what had just happened, but I was on cloud nine. I knew my wife wouldn't be happy when she discovered we were the proud owners of a boat, but I would deal with that later. My friend went with me to pick up my new boat and I stored it at his garage.

I was already convinced that **you could get people to do almost anything if your motives are pure, your rationale convincing and sincere and the interaction takes place in an atmosphere of trust and mutual respect,** but this surprised me. The loan manager decided to trust me, even faced with evidence that maybe he shouldn't. This re-enforced the notion people have a natural inclination to trust, and be helpful, and they will take extraordinary measures on your behalf. Because of the actions of the loan manager, I felt a heightened sense of responsibility to repay the loans. I did not want to create grief for someone who went to such lengths to help me. This was the beginning of a new understanding of the many dynamics involved in a trusting relationship, whether between individuals or leaders and their organizations. These powerful dynamics, treated properly, coupled with the other characteristics of Theory Y leadership, would generate impressive results.

In a strange, twisted sort of way, this experience actually

helped me control my gambling. I was so determined to keep my promise to the loan manager, that I never put the loan payments for the boat or my car at risk on the poker table. This was also the payoff for my wife. She was happy to see me become a little more responsible. In a lot of ways, this relatively small event was life changing. Several months later, we financed a new car purchase through the bank. I paid off the boat and car loans ahead of schedule. I hope the loan manager got a bonus for taking a risk on a customer that obviously, did not meet the bank's standards, but resulted in a profitable transaction.

I had to go to Charlotte, North Carolina to pick up my company car. This was only the second time I had flown. (The first was to Atlanta for the NFA speaking contest). I was still pretty amazed at my good fortune; a great job, a new boat and now a free car; I'm thinking, it doesn't get any better than this! But what really excited me was I knew it would.

I had taken to claims work like a fish to water and had gotten excellent results on several major cases. My trainers and supervisors were impressed with my progress. So in the fall of 1973, I knew it was time for the next step, movement toward my first supervisory position. With the tenure of the people in Richmond, I knew it was not going to happen there in a timeframe consistent with my plan. I discussed it with my wife and decided to ask for a transfer.

It was time for another meeting with my manager. I thanked him for everything he had done, shared with him how great the training had been, told him how much I enjoyed living and working in Richmond, but I needed to leave. He was surprised. I told him I had decided to make insurance my life-long career, that as much as I enjoyed claims work, I wanted to be a manager and I didn't see it happening in Richmond in a timeframe suitable to me, so I would like to be transferred. He understood, but informed me I had been assigned to the Richmond office after training. Normal company rules are transfers after that are associated with promotions, and I was not up for one. I told him I understood, and would be willing to take a lateral transfer to the right place, one with the opportunities I was seeking. After some further discussion, he said he would see what he could do, but warned me not to get my hopes up. I assured him with his connections, I was confident he could make it happen.

Two months went by with no response. Then in the third month he called me into his office and said there was an opening in Des Moines, Iowa, that would be a lateral transfer. I told him I needed to check it out and would get back to him the next day. I found that Des Moines was a lot like Richmond; relatively tame environment with low office turnover. I declined the move.

The holidays passed and 1974 arrived. I was getting restless. Then in late January, my manager called me in again. A claims rep position had opened in the Newark, New Jersey office. He couldn't see why anyone would consider a lateral move from Richmond, Virginia to Newark, New Jersey, but the job was there if I wanted it. I told him that I would investigate and let him know the next day. I made some calls and learned Newark was considered one of the toughest claims environments in the country. In addition to the bad economy and high crime rate, the schools were terrible, and corruption was rampant. Because of these conditions, turnover was very high in the office.

Then I heard the good news, the manager was considered an up and comer, likely to be president of the company one day. He had recently taken over the office to try to turn things around. This sounded too good to be true. This was exactly what I was looking for, a place to have an impact and form a relationship that could be extremely helpful over the coming years. I accepted the job. It was said, I was the only person in the history of the company to accept a lateral transfer into the Newark office! I was an instant celebrity.

My wife was also excited about moving to New Jersey, since her only sister lived in South Jersey, and her favorite uncle lived in East Orange, which is just up the hill from Newark. Two weeks before I reported to Newark we got an all-expense paid trip to find an apartment. We ended up in a comfortable two-bedroom on the seventh floor of a very nice building on South Munn Ave., in East Orange.

When I told the family we were leaving I got a mixed

reaction. My sisters were delighted but my mother was crushed. She said she was prepared for me possibly going into the army, and maybe being transferred, but never thought I would leave home voluntarily. I assured her I was a mere phone call away. Soon the movers showed up, packed our limited belongings and we were on the way to New Jersey. I hitched my gorgeous boat behind our almost new 1973 Pontiac Grand Prix, white on white, and off we went.

MY FIRST MENTOR

I was already a celebrity in Newark, being the only person in the history of the company to take a lateral transfer there, but I decided to make an entrance anyway. I headed to the Aetna office in downtown Newark with my boat still in tow. Since I hadn't met any of the people in the office, I wanted to introduce myself and let them know I had arrived. The office was located on Main Street and the claims department was on the third floor, facing Main. I pulled my car and boat into a no parking zone right in front of the office and activated my flashers. I felt reasonably safe since I doubted anyone in the city could tow a car with a boat attached.

I made my way to the third floor and asked for my new boss. The young lady asked my name, and as soon as people heard it, I was surrounded. They really did want to see this strange person who would leave the security of a place like Richmond, Virginia for the dangers offered up by Newark, and possibly figure out what my motives might be. After introductions all around, I was ushered in to see the boss. He was in his mid-thirties, clean cut, well dressed and very energetic. I knew from my research he was a Penn State graduate and loyal Nittany Lion fan. As first impressions go, he impressed me and I felt almost an immediate connection. Like me, his motive for being in Newark was to further his career. He welcomed me to Newark, said he had heard a lot about me and was glad to have me aboard. We chatted for several minutes, and I decided I really liked him. I then said that I should probably leave since I was parked in a no-parking zone in front of the building. We walked over to his window and looked down on the street. A strange expression came over his face as he turned and asked "Is that your car and boat parked on the street?" I said, "yes." He laughed and said I was the only claim rep he knew that owned a boat. After filling him in on all the particulars, I offered to take him for a ride someday. He said he would like that. We shook hands and I told him I would see him in two days.

As I rode down the elevator, I was all grins. Mission accomplished! It could not have gone any better. I made the impression I wanted to make, a force to be reckoned with, and I really liked my boss and felt we hit it off. It would be great to form a relationship with a potential strong, influential ally and work with somebody who understood exactly what I aimed to accomplish, because he was trying to do the same thing.

The next day, after doing some unpacking, we headed to South Jersey. I had arranged to keep my boat at my sister-in-law's house in Willingboro, New Jersey, just a few miles from the Rancocas Creek, a popular boating spot. Over the coming months we would spend many weekends cruising the Rancocas Creek and picnicking on its secluded beaches. My wife enjoyed the boat as much as I, since it gave her the opportunity to hang out with her sister in a pretty cool setting.

That Monday I arrived in the Newark office for the beginning of my new adventure. Newark was everything I had heard and more. The city was crowded, busy, and in some areas, dangerous. We were not allowed to go into some sections. The office was much bigger than Richmond and appeared to be disorganized and chaotic. The Richmond office ran like a well-oiled machine; Newark appeared to struggle to stay afloat. My new supervisor, a veteran claims man, had spent his entire career in Newark. He was very conservative, strictly by the book and had no aspirations beyond his current position.

As an outside claim rep, I was required to come into the office just one day a week. This was largely driven by the cost and availability of parking spaces. The other days I spent in the field investigating losses or at home doing paper work. I was assigned a block of files left by the person I replaced, who left under suspicious circumstances. My first job was to review each file with my supervisor, determine the current status, get each up to date, and put a plan in place for disposition. This meant spending the first three weeks in the office.

Working from home was new for me, but managing my time was easy. I had plenty of work to keep me busy, and my supervisor kept tight controls over the activities of his claim reps. The claims were like those we had in Richmond. The big difference was the environment. Witnesses were difficult to track down and often distrusted insurance companies, making cooperation rare. We had to be very creative, in most cases, to get the information we needed to settle cases. My research skills came in handy.

I quickly gained a reputation as a very good claim rep, with excellent investigative skills, very good file documentation and the ability to negotiate good settlements. This gave me a lot of access to the boss, who was thrilled to have someone who cared about the work. It also afforded me the opportunity to help train other less experienced claim reps, a task I truly enjoyed.

My first few months in Newark were pretty routine. My boss was working hard to get the place in shape and frequently asked my advice on issues. He was always interested in how things were done in Richmond, and very receptive to my suggestions for changes in Newark. He was probably not a Theory Y practitioner, but he certainly exhibited some of the characteristics, particularly in his dealings with me. I was a willing partner, and took the opportunity to forge a strong bond with him. Our relationship also gave me the chance to get more involved in the management/leadership of the department, a tremendous learning opportunity. This made my supervisor uncomfortable, but he had no choice in the matter.

Even though branch offices were run pretty autonomously, to insure consistency across the company they were still subject to certain company procedures. In addition, claim handling was highly regulated by state governments, and violations could be costly. The home office would conduct periodic audits to insure companywide compliance. I had been in Newark for almost a year when my first audit experience took place. When I told my boss I was looking forward to the team's visit, he was surprised and asked why, since most people dreaded these visits. I told him I was confident in and proud of the work that I did on my files and welcomed the scrutiny from home office so they could see the excellent work I did. He replied that in all of his years in the claims business, he had never heard that response from a claim rep. He applauded my thinking and wished more people approached their work the same way. I got high marks from the audit team and my relationship with the boss grew stronger. The office did better than in previous audits, so he was making progress, and was pleased with the results.

During this time, I encountered organized crime for the first time. Aetna provided bonds for a very large national appliance manufacturer with vast warehousing facilities just outside of Newark. Our bonds covered theft. Over a period of several months, numerous truck-loads of appliances were high jacked. I was assigned the case. I began my investigation the usual way, getting police and FBI reports, visiting the various warehouse facilities and interviewing employees, police officers and FBI agents. I was near to concluding my investigation, but needed the statement of one more officer. I was at the precinct in a conference room, waiting for the officer to arrive, when another officer entered the room, closed the door, got uncomfortably close to me, and suggested I leave. He said they thought I had asked enough questions and no more information would be forth coming. I should settle the claim and move on while I still could.

I left immediately, went straight to the office and reported what happened to my boss. We had been alerted to the likely involvement of organized crime, so we were not totally surprised. We convened a meeting with the home office experts, and much to my relief, they decided to settle the case with the information we had. I moved on. This was a stark example of the difficulty of the Newark claim's environment.

After my first year in Newark I was promoted to senior claim representative. I got a raise and was feeling pretty good about things. But I was getting antsy. Though I enjoyed claim handling, and Newark was an exciting place to work, it was not my goal.

Aetna had a very thorough performance management employee appraisal process. At least once a year each employee's supervisor would assess prior year's performance and set expectations for the coming years. It also included areas of development for your current position, future positions and a plan to get you there. I had my first appraisal after being in Newark a little over a year. I indicated I wanted to move into a position in Marketing and would like to do it on the West Coast. Even though I had never been to California, I thought it would be a great experience working there.

By this time my relationship with my boss was solid and I had discussed my career aspirations with him several times. He was very supportive and committed to helping in any way he could, with the caveat that Aetna's traditional approach was to promote within departments, so moving to another department was possible, but rare.

Around this time I received a new claim that involved a fatality. Our insured, a nineteen-year old, driving a corvette, hit and killed a bicyclist. I had handled numerous fatalities before so there was nothing unusual about the assignment. I conducted my investigation, including diagrams, pictures, police reports, interviews with witnesses and background information on our driver and the victim. In third-party claims companies establish reserves, which represent an estimate of what we think the case is worth, based on the information we have. The reserve amount on serious cases is established by the supervisor, the manager and usually one or two other senior claim representatives. The idea is to get input from the most experienced experts to make the reserve as accurate as possible. In this case, we put up a reserve of $250,000.

The final settlement amount is based on the value of the claim plus an assessment of the liability of the various parties. For example, if we felt the case value was $250,000 and our policy holder was 100% responsible for the accident, we would pay $250,000. If we thought the victim contributed to the accident, the value would be reduced by the amount of that contribution. In other words, if we thought the victim was 25% responsible, the value would be reduced by $62,500. This accident occurred at an uncontrolled intersection which always presents difficult liability situations. However, nineteen year olds driving Corvettes can present even bigger problems, particularly, in the event of a lawsuit.

Not unexpectedly, the family of the victim hired an attorney. Like all good claim reps, I researched the attorney to see what we would be up against. The skills/reputation of the attorney can have a significant effect on what companies are willing to pay. My research revealed this attorney was a rookie, fresh out of law school, and probably a family friend. Shortly after I completed most of my work, I called the attorney and asked if I could come by to discuss the case. He agreed.

I arrived at his office with all of the information I had developed, including a complete analysis of the laws governing intersections. I shared everything with the attorney, something we normally didn't do, but I sensed an opportunity. He was impressed with my work. I concluded with him that this was a tragedy in every respect, but there were significant issues with liability. After a lengthy discussion, he asked me how much I would pay to settle the case. I said, it was much too early to begin those discussions. He persisted, saying hypothetically, what would you pay. I finally said, given all the issues with the case, I would pay $15,000, just to avoid a lawsuit. I reminded him it was not an official offer to settle, and returned to my office. I didn't think much about the case after I left his office. Two days later the attorney called me and said, "Mr. Austin, my clients will accept your offer of $15,000 to settle this case". I didn't want to appear too anxious, so I reminded him that wasn't an offer, but with his assurance his clients would sign a full release, I could make it happen. He said they would. I agreed to settle.

I was beyond excited, and rushed into the office to get a check and release before he changed his mind. I couldn't wait to tell my supervisor and my boss. This was BIG. My excitement was quickly dashed when I told my supervisor. He said, "You can't do that; $15,000 is over your authority and requires my approval". Claim reps were given authority levels, amounts they could pay without further approvals, based on their experience. Mine was $5,000. He said we had a huge problem and needed to go see the boss right away. Authority violations were serious and could result in some disciplinary action. I was crushed. I was expecting high fives and a bonus, and he was threatening termination. We grabbed the file and headed to see the boss. My supervisor said, "We have a big problem. Al has just exceeded his authority and settled our bicycle case for $15,000."The boss almost leaped out of his chair and said," You're right; it's going to be difficult to decide how big his bonus should be". Then the celebration began.

I learned several valuable lessons from this. First, you never want authority levels to prevent people from making good decisions. There are two types of authority; those you are granted and those you take. If you have competent, well-trained people, you want them to make good business decisions in the best interest of the company, regardless of authority levels. Recognizing this requires a high degree of **TRUST**. It is always better to beg forgiveness than ask permission. Failure to see the big picture can result in disastrous consequences. My supervisor saw an authority violation. My boss saw a $235,000 savings for the company. It is highly likely my failure to act could have cost the company $235,000.

Newark was going as planned. The five P's were delivering as expected and I was making significant progress toward my goals. I was discovering how dynamic each of the P's were, which re-enforced their importance. My one surprise was the relative importance of **PROACTIVITY**. It is quite likely I would still be behind a desk, in Richmond, Virginia handling small claims if I had not taken the initiative in getting the outside claim rep's job and the transfer to Newark. I did, however, have to be prepared to take advantage of both, which re-enforced the importance of **PREPARATION** and **PERFORMANCE**. I had learned a lot in the short time I had been in Newark, and my relationship with my boss was even better than I had hoped.

About a month after the bicycle case settled, my boss

called me into his office, and asked how much I knew about Aetna's National Accounts Department. I replied I knew they were responsible for large commercial accounts, but little else. He explained the National Accounts Department, aka, NAD was the brain-child of two Aetna senior executives, looking for a more efficient way to handle large commercial accounts. It was created just three years prior and was a unique model in the insurance industry. The impetus behind its creation was the special needs of very large, complicated accounts that required a level of expertise beyond the normal business flow. Aetna distributed all of its products through independent agents and brokers, but the NAD model called for direct relationships between the company and the insureds/policy holders, not to the exclusion of the agent, but jointly. This direct contact required a staff of highly skilled account handlers to act as service coordinators for all aspects of the account's needs. The regular company departments, claims, underwriting, loss control and marketing, still provided services but the account handlers design programs, negotiate terms, conditions and premiums, and coordinate service delivery.

    NAD consisted of a home office support structure, and nine field offices located in Boston, New York, Philadelphia, Charlotte, Atlanta, Huston, St. Louis, Cleveland and Los Angeles. Each field office is staffed with a NAD Team consisting of an account supervisor, and account representative from each discipline, claims, underwriting and loss control, and a manager. Each account handler is required to provide the technical expertise for his or her field and become proficient enough in the other disciplines to handle accounts, on a day-to-day basis. Account handlers worked directly with the Risk Managers, CFO's and occasionally CEO's of client companies. This required the utmost in professionalism, knowledge, confidence and communication skills.

    He said NAD's current manager/leader, was his friend and mentor. They are looking to fill an account representative position in the Los Angeles office with someone with a claims background. The selection process is rigorous and very competitive.

NAD jobs are considered glamour positions because of the size accounts they handle and the territories they cover. The Los Angeles office handles the thirteen western states. Frequent travel and entertaining are involved, so luxury hotels and high end restaurants are normal fare, all covered by expense account.

There is one potential drawback. NAD is a relatively new concept with an unproven track record. It is out of the mainstream of the company. From a long term career prospective, re-entry may be difficult.

He said that he would recommend me if the Los Angeles position interested me. I was so excited I could hardly speak. This was literally too good to be true. A job that would give me the generalist training I needed for my long term goals, working in California, traveling throughout the entire west coast, staying at the best hotels, eating at the best restaurants and rubbing elbows with some of the most influential corporate leaders in the country. I knew from my claim work that among others, we insured Boeing, Morrison Knudsen Construction Company, one of the top three in the world, Westin International Hotels, Universal Studios, and Bechtel Engineering and Construction.

My boss sensed my excitement and reiterated the difficulty of the selection process and the long term career risk. I told him I would take my chances with the process, and thought the benefits of working in this kind of operation far outweighed the long term career risk. I asked him to make the call. (After all, I knew I could get people to do almost anything if my motives were pure and my rationale convincing and sincere, and the discussion occurred in an atmosphere of trust and mutual respect).

A few days later, my boss gave me the name and phone number of a person to call in the home office to arrange a visit. I made the call and set up a series of four interviews.

The next week I traveled to the home office for just my second visit. It was still impressive and somewhat intimidating, made all the more so because of the purpose. I was last there for training with no significant consequences based on performance. This time, my future hung in the balance.

I didn't know any of the interviewers, but found them

knowledgeable, a little intense, and focused on their mission. The questions involved my upbringing, my educational background, technical claim questions, including large claims I handled, my interest in NAD and why I felt I was a good fit for such a challenging position. I was well-prepared and answered every question without hesitation and with the utmost confidence. My background in dealing with people and my comfort in communicating in pressure situations had prepared me well for this. At the end of the day, the four interviewers took me to dinner. My guess is evaluating my social graces was a part of the process. At the end, they told me several people were being considered for the position, and they would narrow the list to three next week and notify me if I was a finalist. If so, I would come back to Hartford to meet with the head of NAD, who would make the final decision. I expressed my appreciation for their time and interest in me and said good-night. I was staying at the Sheraton Hotel in downtown Hartford, but got little sleep that night.

The next morning I drove back to Newark, bursting with anticipation. I wanted this job, maybe a little more than I should have. I wasn't sure how I would deal with rejection. I was, however, pleased with my performance at the interviews and felt I had given myself the best chance possible.

The next few days passed slowly, but I got the call! I had an interview scheduled with the MAN in two days!

My boss gave me a very valuable tip when dealing with the head of NAD, a big man, imposing figure, with a personality bigger than life, that could be intimidating to the faint of heart, and would not hesitate to use this to gather information he needed to make a decision. His advice was ignore the bluster, be yourself and you'll be fine. Since I was not prone to intimidation, this didn't cause me any concern. I was prepared!

I arrived in the home office a little early the day of my interview. I bumped into two of the guys that conducted my prior interviews. We chatted for a few minutes, exchanged pleasantries and they wished me good luck with the Big Guy.

I was sitting in a conference room when he arrived. Six-feet three at 250 pounds, he had a baritone voice that could shatter glass. (I found out later his nickname was "The Boomer.") He had an air of confidence that came dangerously close to arrogance and left no question he was the boss. My first thought was this is going to be interesting, and I was looking forward to the test I knew I was about to face.

After a little small talk, he asked how I ended up at Aetna. I told him, I was recruited by the Richmond office as a part of the Affirmative Action initiative, had really planned to stay for a year because I was going to law school after my wife found a job, but fell in love with the business and decided to make it my career. This was the first time I had shared my original intent with anyone in the company. He asked how he could be assured I wouldn't change my mind in six months, and head to law school? I told him he couldn't, except for my word. I said if I had planned to leave Aetna I would not have taken a lateral transfer from a safe job in Richmond, Virginia to one with the challenge of Newark, New Jersey. He said, "Good point," and I knew I had passed the first test.

He was intrigued by my background and had a number of questions about my family. He was impressed with my work history in college, both working with the ladies, (a story he found hard to believe) and M & B Headwear. He actually said, if I could talk Dr. Bell into giving me that job, I could probably talk anybody into doing almost anything. I didn't share my mantra with him, but he could tell, I thought I could. He knew how well I had performed in Newark so he was comfortable with my technical abilities in the claims business, but questioned my grasp of the other disciplines. I acknowledged I knew very little about the premium development side of underwriting, but was very comfortable with our contracts, since most claim handling required the interpretation of policy language to reach the appropriate settlement amount. I also told him I had a general idea of our loss control department and had worked with them on several claims. I assured him I was a quick study and would close my knowledge gap fast. I also told him I had great communication skills, was comfortable in pressure situations and would bring a level of enthusiasm to the position I doubted he had seen before.

After about a two hour session, he took me to lunch, where he told me about NAD, its mission, his aspirations for the organization, where he thought they were in their development, the threats to their long-term success and his optimistic view of the future. The early review of the model indicated it was working very well. The brokers were still a little nervous about our direct contact with their clients, but the clients loved it so the brokers would adjust. He thought the NAD field structure and team concept were also on target. An additional office or two may have to be added down the road, but coverage right now was sufficient. One issue still being debated was how much cross training the account handlers should have. Some thought they should become experts in each discipline, a herculean training task, while others felt, with expert backup, generalist knowledge sufficed. Right now he was content to let it evolve naturally. He predicted NAD would be wildly successful and that other companies would try to duplicate our model.

Lunch was very pleasant. We shook hands and he said I would hear in the next two days about the position. They would call, even if I was not selected, which I thought was a nice touch. He also said he enjoyed our meeting and thought I handled it well. I headed back to Newark. I barely remember the drive back. My head was spinning. I didn't want to get too excited, but I thought the meeting went very well. I didn't know the other candidates, so it was a little difficult to gage the outcome. The one thing I did know, when I reflected on the meeting, there wasn't a single thing I would have done differently. That rarely happens, but is always a good sign.

The next two days passed slowly. I made it a point to be in the office both days because I wanted to be nearby when the answer came. On the second day, the boss called me to his office. I could tell from the look on his face, I had won the job. I think he was almost as happy as I. He knew this was a huge step in my career. This also was my first step in gaining the generalist knowledge that is the linchpin of Theory Y leadership. Later that day I got a call from my new boss at NAD, welcoming me to his organization and giving some more details about my job.

My position in Los Angeles would be account representative, a class 30, normally supervisory, but an exception for NAD because of the complexity of the work. I would receive a raise and a cost of living differential because of the higher cost of living in Los Angeles. My supervisor would be Richard Ioset and the office manager was Howard Marsh, a Texan. The office handled some of NAD's largest accounts, including Boeing, Westin International Hotels, and Sisters of Providence Hospitals, headquartered in Seattle, Washington, Longview Fiber, located in Longview, Washington, Universal Studios, located in Los Angeles, Clorox, headquartered in Oakland, California, Morrison Knudsen Construction Company headquartered in Boise, Idaho and Hensel Phelps Construction Company headquartered in Greely, Colorado. The LA team logged more flight time than any other, so I should be prepared to spend a lot of time traveling. After a month in LA I would return to the home office for a week of orientation.

My wife was excited about the move to Los Angeles. She had enjoyed the time in New Jersey, on the water with her sister, but the chance to live out west was appealing.

We decided not to take a pre-move trip to Los Angeles; instead, the company would put us up in temporary housing until we found a place. Some research of the area and the fact we had a boat convinced us living near the water would be ideal.

We had been in New Jersey less than fifteen months when, in mid-November, 1975, the movers arrived to pack our belongings. We had decided to drive to LA. Neither of us had been west of Chicago, so we thought it would be a good opportunity to see the country. After getting the boat, we would drive to Virginia to spend a few days with the family before heading west. I also had to figure out how to get the boat to California.

We spent two days saying our goodbyes. As luck would have it, a friend of mine was attending a Shriner's convention in Los Angeles in January and he and his wife had decided to drive their RV across country. He volunteered to bring my boat with him, a generous offer I couldn't refuse.

We were set and off we went!

GO WEST YOUNG MAN

We decided to take the southern route and follow old Route 66 as much as possible. Because we wanted to see as much as we could, we planned to take five to seven days. There was no rush to get to Los Angeles and we needed some time to decompress, reflect, and get rejuvenated for this new experience. Moving nearly three thousand miles from home, to a city where neither of us had been and didn't know a single person, was a bit nerve-wracking and we needed to be prepared. We planned to stop at several places along the route and at Flagstaff, Arizona, head north to the Grand Canyon and Las Vegas. We stopped in Nashville, Tennessee, Little Rock, Arkansas, Amarillo, Texas and Albuquerque, New Mexico. The stops went fine, but when we arrived in Flagstaff, there was a major snow storm so we decided to stay south and continue on to Los Angeles.

We arrived in Los Angeles on a Friday, and checked into the hotel near downtown. I decided to wait until Monday to contact the office and spend the week end exploring. Los Angeles was unlike any other big city I'd visited. There was really no distinguishable downtown and it seemed to go on forever. We headed for the beach and ended up in Santa Monica. A ride up and down the coast highway, from Malibu to Marina Del Rey, convinced us that this was the place to be. With a little checking, we found Malibu and Marina Del Rey were out of our price range, but we could afford Santa Monica, and it was only five miles from Marina Del Rey where I could launch the boat.

The rest of the weekend we spent exploring and on Monday I called the real estate agent assigned to help us and told her we wanted a two bedroom apartment in Santa Monica, as close to the beach as possible. She assured me she could do that.

Aetna occupied several floors in the American Cement Building on Wilshire Blvd, across from the famed MacArthur Park. NAD was on the fourth floor. I was greeted by the administrative assistant. It was a small office since there were only five people on the California Team. My new boss rushed over and introduced himself and took me into the manager's office. He welcomed me to the LA team. I then met the other members, the underwriting supervisor and the loss control supervisor.

From our first hand shake, I could tell the loss control man was not glad to see me. In a few days, he made it known he felt the only reason I got the job in NAD was because I was Black and that he would do little to help me because I was destined to fail. Though surprised by his attitude, I was always ready for this reaction. I told him since I didn't anticipate needing his help he didn't have to worry about me asking for it. My mother had prepared me for him, years ago, and while I sympathized with his plight, I had no intension of letting it interfere with my plans.

The underwriting supervisor was very pleasant and he and I hit it off immediately. This was good because his expertise was what I needed the most, since I knew little about underwriting. My new supervisor was undoubtedly one of the nicest people I have ever met in my life, and I felt sure would do anything possible to make my transition as smooth as possible.

After two days, my wife found a comfortable two-bedroom on the second floor of a very nice garden apartment complex in Santa Monica, just four blocks from the beach. Best of all, it had a large garage that would accommodate my boat. She then started her job search. In a matter of days, she landed a job with the Santa Monica school board just ten minutes from home. Things were falling into place nicely and we were already feeling good about our new home.

I spent the first few weeks in LA with my new colleagues reviewing the accounts handled by the office and the procedural manuals governing the operation. Even though the loss control supervisor was suspicious of me being there, he was not openly hostile. I think my initial response surprised him and he wasn't sure what to think. Each of the supervisors handled two or three large accounts and several smaller ones to round out their work load. My supervisor had the Morrison Knudsen Construction Company, headquartered in Boise, Idaho, Sisters of Providence hospital chain, headquartered in Seattle, Washington and Longview Fiber, a paper company, headquartered in Longview, Washington. The underwriting supervisor worked with Universal Studios, headquartered in Los Angeles, Clorox, headquartered in Oakland, California, and Bechtel, headquartered in Orange County, California. Loss control had Boeing, headquartered in Seattle, Washington, and Aetna's largest single account, First National Bank of Utah, headquartered in Salt Lake City, Utah, Westin International Hotels, headquartered in Seattle, Washington and Hensel Phelps Construction Company, headquartered in Greely, Colorado. These accounts paid us between two and twenty million dollars a year in premium and required a lot of attention.

After about six weeks in LA, I returned to Hartford for my orientation, where I would learn about the support operation in the home office, with particular emphasis on the various underwriting programs. I was looking forward to this because I was eager to learn.

My visit started with an introduction to the NAD staff, including the responsibilities each handled. The head man was his usual over-powering self and I couldn't decide how I felt about him. He was obviously talented, but with his staff projected an air of intimidation that I felt stifled the candid feedback leaders needed. There was a director of claims administration, a director of engineering, loss control and a director of underwriting. Each director provided support and technical assistance to the field teams and occasionally visited accounts. The NAD managers reported to a vice-president of operations. I got a good overview of each operation and how it could be helpful to the field teams.

During my second day in the home office I had some time to kill between sessions so I wandered around the halls. I walked by Ollie Patrell's office. Mr. Patrell was the head of the entire Commercial Lines Division, and the head of NAD reported to him. I knew this only because I had seen his name on numerous company documents. I stuck my head into Mr. Patrell's outer office and asked his secretary if he was in. She looked a little surprised, but said yes, "Why do you ask?" I told her I was in for orientation from the LA National Accounts team, and just wanted to introduce myself to Mr. Patrell. She asked if he was expecting me and I said, no. She was a very nice lady and said, let me check to see if Mr. Patrell has time to say hello and disappeared into his office. In just a few minutes she emerged and said, "Mr. Patrell will see you now".

When I walked in, Mr. Patrell greeted me like we were old friends. I introduced myself and said what a pleasure it was to meet him. He insisted I call him Ollie. Then we had a very pleasant conversation about my background, my early impressions of NAD and his assessment of how the model was working. He was very optimistic about the future of NAD and thought our model would become the standard for the industry in years to come. At noon he called his secretary and asked if he had a lunch appointment, and she said no. He took me to lunch, where our conversation continued.

As I left Ollie I couldn't believe that I had just spent almost two hours with the head of the division and he had taken me to lunch. I was also sure I had made a favorable impression and he would not forget my name. I expected this connection was going to pay dividends at some point in the future, and I was not mistaken. This was my path back to the mainstream of the company, the long-term threat my Newark manager had cautioned me about. I liked Ollie, and was impressed he would take the time to get to know me.

It was hard for me to concentrate that afternoon, but I managed. I knew my contact with Ollie would be useless if I didn't perform in LA and the material I was about to cover during the rest of my visit was critical. I was about to learn what separated national accounts from the rest of Aetna's business and why they were so important.

The law of large numbers does not apply to national accounts. In our standard business, we expect each homogeneous group to be profitable with little regard for the profitability of any individual account. Because of the size of the premium for national accounts, and the severity of the exposures, we expect each one to stand on its own and produce a profit for the company. The theory is large accounts should pay their normal and expected losses as a cost of doing business and buy protection for the catastrophic exposure that could jeopardize their balance sheet. So the insurance company's role is to work with each account to design a funding mechanism for the normal and expected losses and insurance coverage above an appropriate self-funding level. These programs are collectively referred to as loss responsive or retrospective rated programs. There are several different designs, but they all accomplish the same purpose.

In addition to providing catastrophic protection and program design, the insurance company also provides all of the services necessary to support the account's program. We handle all of the claims, usually with some oversight from the account, and conduct inspections of job sites, factories or any other premises and make recommendations for safety and quality control. When you are self-funding losses, loss control takes on a whole new meaning.

The two most popular loss responsive programs are retrospective rated programs and large deductibles. Under retrospective plans the company estimates the amount of claims payments for a twelve month period and the account pays a quarterly premium based on that estimate plus the expenses to handle the claims and provide the excess insurance coverage. At some point in the future, usually eighteen months, an accounting is done and adjustments made based on the actual results; either a return premium to the account or an additional premium charge.

Under a large deductible plan, the account selects a loss level it's comfortable with, based on past claim experience, and agrees to pay all claims up to that amount. The company then handles those claims and bills the account, on a monthly basis, for the amount of the payments, plus the cost of handling the losses. There is also a charge for the insurance protection above the deductible.

The NAD team is responsible for working with the

broker and the account to design the program best suited for the accounts' operation and financial position. They are also responsible for designing and coordinating all of the services required to support the program. This requires countless hours of negotiations to put the program in place and daily involvement in the supporting services. Claim settlement amounts are frequently disputed, and NAD's role is to resolve them in a manner that protects the Aetna's interest and keeps the account happy, a tightrope walk that can get dicey at times, and requires the utmost in diplomacy.

The contracts outlining coverage and exclusions start with the basic insurance contract used for all commercial accounts. However, because of the size and complexity of national accounts, these contracts are modified to fit the specific needs and exposures of individual accounts. This is done with endorsements, or amendments, to the basic contract that either expand or exclude coverage. As with any contract, when a loss occurs, the interpretation of the intent of the parties can be contentious.

I learned a lot during my week in the Home Office and was anxious to return to LA to put it into practice. I also made another valuable connection that would be instrumental in achieving my long term goals.

Shortly after I returned to LA I made my first account visit with my supervisor. We went to Seattle to conduct a claim review with the Sisters of Providence, and discuss the upcoming contract renewal. This account was written on a large deductible and scrutinized claim payments very closely. The agent for the account was Rahn & Company, a family owned agency that handled the account for the past fifty years. We had a very good relationship with the account and the agent, so the meeting went quite well. I got my first glimpse at the importance of relationships in the large account business, and how critical it was to be able to respond immediately to questions and concerns. Accounts paying ten million dollars a year for insurance didn't want to deal with messengers, but decision makers. We answered all of their claim questions and got the information we needed for the renewal.

Back in the office, I spent as much time with the underwriting supervisor as I could. As the underwriting expert, he could help re-enforce what I learned in the home office, and provide the practical application that I needed to become fluent enough to conduct client meetings solo. He was very willing to share his knowledge and happy to have a willing student.

It became obvious very quickly that Dick, my boss, and Howard, the manager, didn't have a good relationship. The manager felt my supervisor should have been more proficient in all of the disciplines. The tension between the two created some anxious moments for me. I needed to show my progress and avoid putting my supervisor in an awkward position. I thought he was too nice to deal with the manager, who could be a bully, and this would probably end badly.

My next client visit was with the underwriting supervisor to Universal Studios, where we conducted a claims review, led by me, and toured the facilities for my benefit. Universal was our glamour account. We got to hang out on the various sound stages and occasionally watch the filming of a movie or TV show. The risk manager enjoyed showing off their facility and bragging about the latest project. We had a very good relationship with the account and the visit went quite well. The account enjoyed the attention we gave them. We always made it a point to visit all of our accounts periodically, even if only to take the risk manager to lunch. These feel-good meetings always made the tougher business meetings easier.

The account we had the biggest issues with was Hensel Phelps Construction Company. Unhappy with our services, they threatened to move their business to another company. The large commercial account business was very competitive with companies knocking on the doors of our accounts, promising to save them loads of money and deliver superior services. Much to my surprise, the supervisor asked me to accompany him on his next account visit, where the risk manager was also the general counsel. The account was written on a retrospective plan, and claim settlements and reserves were a constant issue. Being an attorney, he was never happy with our handling, so I was cautioned to be ready for a battle. To me, this sounded like it could be fun. I was very comfortable with the claim side of the business and relished the opportunity to defend our position with a worthy opponent.

We arrived in Greely via Denver and immediately knew we were in the home town of Munfort Meat Packaging. The odor was almost unbearable. A local agency, Flood & Peterson, handled the account. They told us the risk manager had received proposals from two of our major competitors and said it was going to be very difficult for him to leave the business with Aetna. We had been dealing with the account for a number of years, and I think frustration got the best of my colleague. He basically said, if that happens, so be it. I could tell the local agents were not happy with his response and sensed that their relationship with us was not good. I said,"Let's meet with the risk manager, get to the root of his concerns, and see if we can alleviate them."

The account's greeting was cool and his handshake with the supervisor perfunctory. When I said I would be conducting the claim review, he asked about my supervisor, who had attended these meetings in the past. I told him I had joined the team to assist with the claim function. He asked about my background, which I gladly shared. There was a bite of tension in the room when I suggested that we get started with the review. There were few claims to discuss, but they were large claims with reserves ranging from a half-million to over a million dollars. On the first claim, the account questioned our interpretation of a clause in the contract covering a construction site loss that occurred in Baltimore, Maryland. He thought we were too liberal, and too willing to spend his money. He laid out the rationale to support his position. I let him continue uninterrupted until he was done. Then I said, "I'm impressed with the work you have put into supporting your position and I can see how you arrived at the decision you did. However, the case law you sighted is not exactly on point, and the jurisdiction does not cover Maryland". I then explained two more relevant cases that did cover Maryland. A healthy discussion over the merits of each position followed, after which he reluctantly agreed that we were probably right. I assured him we would continue to explore every avenue to mitigate the claim payment as much as possible, because contrary to his belief, we did not enjoy spending his money, because an unhappy client was bad business. He said, "You know, you're right."

The next case involved a disagreement over the reserve amount on a very serious case. Naturally, he thought the reserve was too high. We had a heated argument with no resolution in sight. Much to his delight, I finally agreed to lower the reserve. The reserve represented our best guess of the ultimate payment and would impact the account's premium, but only temporary, since the final reckoning would occur after the claim was settled.

We had lively discussions on the rest of the cases with some minor adjustments, but mainly explanations he accepted. As the morning wore on, I could sense him developing a healthy respect for me and at this stage of the game that was enough. After the meeting, he wanted to have lunch at the Greely Country Club, where he and the local agents were members. I rode to lunch with him and he recounted the history of Hensel Phelps and his background with the company. It was a pleasant trip and a good opportunity for me to cultivate my relationship with him.

At the club, I asked him for a suggestion for lunch and he recommended the Monte Cristo sandwich. I had the Monte Cristo sandwich that day and the next ten times I ate at the club.

After lunch, the agent said he thought the meeting went well, but was probably not enough to save the account. We headed back to LA.

Back in the office, I decided it was time for me to become a full member of the team. I felt I was ready to assume responsibility for total account handling, and I knew exactly which account should be my first assignment- Hensel Phelps. So I told the manager I thought I was ready, and I would like to take over the handling of Hensel Phelps. He reminded me of the problems we had with the account. I assured him I was well aware of the problems, had attended a recent meeting with the current supervisor and felt I could save the account. He said that would take a miracle. He called the current supervisor into the office and asked him for his thoughts. He laughed and said that was the most insane thing he had heard recently. I pushed back and said it was not insane; we were in jeopardy of losing the account and if I thought I could save it, what did we have to lose? After a little more discussion, the manager said he would think about it.

The next day he called us into his office. He said he had decided I would have the account, which clearly disturbed the current supervisor. While he might have been relieved that he wouldn't have to deal with Hensel Phelps anymore, the prospect of me saving the account was painful for him to imagine. Nonetheless, he agreed to help make the transition as smooth as possible. I rejected his offer to travel with me to Greely to make the announcement and told him a complete review of the account and our history would be all I needed from him. Despite his feelings about me, I was sure he would always keep the best interest of the company in mind and do whatever he could to help.

This was a major move on my part, and maybe the sternest test yet for the five P's. I had asked for the tough assignment and would now have to hit a home run. I would have to get Hensel Phelps to renew its contract with us in the face of some difficult challenges. I took comfort though, in knowing that **you can get people to do almost anything if your motives are pure, your rationale convincing and sincere, and the discussion takes place in an atmosphere of trust and mutual respect**. The risk manager had no reason to distrust me and I felt our first meeting established a measure of respect that would insure a level playing field. I was cautiously optimistic.

My manager called the agent to inform him of the change. I then called the Flood and Peterson agency and told them we would work hard to restore the trust vital to continuing our relationship with our mutual client, Hensel Phelps. I asked them to arrange a dinner meeting for us with the account so we could get to know each other better and I could get a better feel for the current state of our relationship, what got us there and how we could move forward.

I spent the next week buried in Hensel Phelps files and discussions with the old supervisor. From what I could tell, there were no major issues with the account's program, but significant issues with the parties involved. They didn't like each other which made minor issues, when they arose, difficult to resolve. There had been several disputes over claim handling, but that was not all that uncommon. It seemed to me our relationship with the account was the biggest challenge. I thought this was good news, because if there was one thing I was good at, it was building relationships.

As I prepared for my trip to Greely, the second time in two weeks, I was feeling a bit more optimistic. I had seen that while the risk manager might appear to be a bully, he just enjoys a vigorous debate, and he respects people who have a valid point of view and are willing to fight for it.

Flying into Denver, it occurred to me this was my first solo trip. I had been in LA less than a year, had learned a tremendous amount and now had my first account assignment that could make me an instant hero, if I could save the relationship.

The agent and I met the account at the risk manager's favorite restaurant, a steakhouse with an extensive wine list. Since Greely was the home of Munfort Meat packaging, I was not surprised. It turned out that Joseph Phelps, one of the owners, was a wine connoisseur, owned a small winery in Napa Valley, dabbled in wine making, and always made sure the restaurant's cellar was well-stocked. I made a mental note to pace myself, knowing over indulging could be disastrous. The evening started with the usual small talk. I made sure there was equal time for everyone to share.

Mid-way through the meal, I said this is a business meeting, and we should probably discuss some business. All agreed. I told the risk manager I was taking over handling of the account, and wanted to get to know him better and get a clearer understanding of the state of the relationship. Then I surprised him by saying, "The first thing I need to know is if you are interested in continuing your relationship with Aetna or have you already decided to move your account?". I told him I was not interested in going through a futile exercise that would leave me frustrated and provide him with some sense of retribution for any wrongs he thought he may have suffered. Before he could answer, I said, "If you keep your business with us, I can assure you I will go to the ends of the earth to make sure our relationship is strengthened and you get the level of professional service you deserve". I paused, and he said, "Wow, that was a mouth full!" Then he said, "I appreciate you being up front and laying your cards on the table, and not making grandiose promises before knowing my position or intentions". Then he launched into a lengthy discussion about his lack of respect for the previous man from Aetna who seemed to have no regard for the client's position. He understood our need to make a profit, but given the nature of the program, there was always more than one way to get to the same outcome. His greatest frustration was with that lack of flexibility. Then he ordered two more bottles of wine.

The local agent offered a recent example. A rather large claim had been reserved at a reasonable level for several months, but just prior to the retro adjustment date, we increased the reserve substantially. When asked to wait until after the retro adjustment, we refused. The account said that was a perfect example. This was a cash-flow issue only. We all know when the claim is finalized we're going to pay whatever it cost. Why wouldn't you give us the benefit of the doubt and wait? We are a construction company and cash-flow matters. I then said, "I'm not familiar with this particular case, and cannot comment on our rationale, but I can understand your disappointment, and agree that barring any unusual circumstances, we should be able to accommodate your request." He then said, "All we're asking for is an objective discussion where compromise is possible, if the facts warrant it". I said, "Spoken like a true lawyer."

We had a healthy discussion about several other issues, but none that were deal breakers. I finally said, "You haven't answered my original question." I knew I was pressing the issue, but I wasn't going to end the meeting without an answer.

He then said, "Al, we've had a long relationship with Aetna, over ten years. In addition to our property and casualty coverage, you write all of our bonds. As you are well aware, it's difficult and potentially expensive to move an account of our size. So the answer to your question is no, I don't want to move to another company, but, you're going to have to give me a reason to stay". I said, "Fair enough", and we ordered after dinner drinks.

At the hotel I met with the agents. They both thought dinner went well and felt the account was pleased with the discussions, but cautioned he was very serious about giving him a reason to stay. They said we made a huge step in that direction by assigning the account to me.

I was pleased with how dinner had gone, but knew there was a lot of work to do. My **goal** was clear; **I had to renew the Hensel Phelps contract.** I also knew **"a goal without a plan was just a wish"**, so I had to develop a plan that would give me the best chance to achieve my goal. As I drove back to Denver that morning I was already formulating that plan.

The bond coverage for Hensel Phelps was handled by the Denver branch office, and was by far their largest account. I knew Hensel didn't want to move that coverage. They had a very good relationship with the Denver office and bonding is much more difficult to replace than property and casualty coverage. Few companies can provide the coverage and even fewer could handle an account as big as Hensel Phelps. It is not uncommon, however, for contractors to have their bonds with one company and the P & C with another. In fact, some prefer it that way. As I formulated my plan, I thought it would give me some leverage if I could give Hensel the impression that, from Aetna's perspective, the two were linked, and I thought I knew how to do that.

I called the general manager for Denver, and asked if I could stop in to see him before I flew back to LA. He said sure. I wanted him to attend the renewal meeting. His presence would be highly unusual and I knew he had never gone before. He knew I had already taken over the account and was aware of some of our problems. I asked if he would be willing to attend the renewal meeting as a show of support. He asked if I wanted to make the continuation of the bond coverage contingent on the P & C renewal. I said absolutely not. I told him I understood the importance and profitability of the account to the branch and would never do anything to jeopardize that. I just want to show a united front and let him do the rest. Since it was unusual for the general manager to attend a renewal meeting, I was sure it would be seen as a move above and beyond to keep the account with

Aetna. He agreed to attend.

Back in LA, I briefed my manager on dinner and shared with him my plan to include the Denver manager in the renewal meeting. He thought this was a good idea and offered to attend. Not wanting to hurt his feelings, I told him the theme of the meeting was going to be "New Faces, New Beginnings" and with all due respect, he didn't qualify. He understood.

The next week I spent hours going through Hensel Phelps' program with our underwriting supervisor. I wanted to make sure there were no short comings. The program was solid, but there are always tweaks that can be made. After all, the only constant is what's going to be paid; the variables are when and how. Working with the home office underwriters, we came up with a few things that would give the account a little more cash-flow. I also invited the home office underwriting manager to attend the renewal meeting. This was usual procedure, but he hadn't been to Greely in several years.

With the branch on board and the underwriting program tweaked, I turned my attention to claims. The account had made it clear that last minute reserve changes, just prior to the retro adjustment, were unacceptable. Aetna was not going to alter its reserving practices, but I thought we could control the timing. I called my claim support person in the home office. After a long discussion, we came up with a simple solution I thought would work. We would conduct a thorough review of all claims with the account three months prior to the retro adjustment. Whatever reserves resulted from that review would not change prior to the retro adjustment, unless there was a settlement, in which case the settlement amount would be reflected. The claim department may not be happy with this, but this time, the preservation of client satisfaction would take precedence over the strict application of a policy, whose ultimate intent would remain unchanged.

The renewal meeting was set and I was ready. I felt good about what we had put together and confident we would give Hensel Phelps a reason to stay with Aetna. I was heading to Greely via Denver for the third time in six weeks. I was so far away from the farm the memories were fading, but not the lessons

I learned from the experience. Teamwork, collaboration, candor, respect and trust were just as important in LA and Greely as they were on the farm.

The local agent opened the meeting with introductions, including the home office underwriting manager. Then I announced the meeting theme of "New Faces, New Beginnings". They liked it and I knew we were off to a good start. The meeting went very well, almost anti-climatic after all of the pre-meeting build-up, but I credit that to excellent **preparation**. Everybody there knew his role and played it exceptionally well. After a short two hours we adjourned to the Greely Country Club, where I had my usual Monte Cristo sandwich. Lunch ended with the account's toast to our relationship and his decision to remain with Aetna. I could barely restrain myself and almost hugged him. He certainly knew the importance of the renewal to Aetna, but had no idea how important it was to me personally. I had asked for the tough assignment, and **HIT A HOME RUN!**

Back in LA the celebration started before I returned. Everyone was delighted we kept the business and all but the past supervisor was happy for me. He was shocked and had no idea how to process what happened. Believe it or not, it didn't change his stated position that the only reason I got the job was because of my color. Since this was his problem, it didn't dampen my spirits one bit. I actually felt sorry for him. He obviously had some inner demons affecting him far more than anything I ever did.

My wife and I celebrated with dinner at Scandia, one of the fanciest restaurants in Los Angeles. She had lived with my anxiety over the last six weeks, knowing that I had to hit a home run, and not at all sure that I could. I think she was as relieved as I was and happy that things worked out the way they did.

Two days later the boss called me into his office, congratulated me again for the Phelps renewal and said how pleased he was with my progress since arriving in LA. He then said he was planning an unusual move and wanted to discuss it with me first. His plan was to demote my supervisor to account representative and promote me with him reporting to me. I was shocked, but without hesitation said, "That won't work," he has been too good to me both professionally and personally for me to participate in something that would be, at a minimum, embarrassing to him. As much as I would love the promotion, I was prepared to wait for a better opportunity. I don't think he was completely surprised.

My wife is the only person that knew about that conversation. My supervisor and his wife had invited us to dinner at their home several times. We kind of thought of them as our parents away from home and they were always more than willing to accommodate. My wife said she was proud of me for not letting greed and ambition cloud my judgment.

The next couple of months were action packed. I was busy putting the Hensel Phelps renewal to bed and working on writing a new account. NAD was responsible for writing new business. A national broker who handled Universal Studios had called me about writing the coverage for a German crane company, Liebherr. One of the largest crane manufacturers in Europe, they were moving into the United States. They were headquartered in Norfolk, Virginia, but the insurance would be handled out of LA. It was not a huge account, two million dollars, but was expected to grow rapidly and needed a national company like Aetna to handle its growth. Since we were well-known in the construction business, we had the inside track.

A few months after I had had the conversation with the boss, my supervisor asked me to take a walk with him. He told me he was going to resign. His relationship with our manager was beyond repair and he had an opportunity to take a job with Johnson & Higgins, at the time one of the largest brokers in the country. It gave him the opportunity to move back to Idaho and now that his kids were grown, he and his wife were looking forward to going back home. He was going to submit his resignation that day, but wanted to give me a heads-up. I told him I understood, thanked him for all he had done for me and wished him well in his new endeavors. He had learned about my earlier conversation with the boss, thanked me for what I had done, and said he was sure I had a great career ahead.

The day after his resignation as supervisor, the manager

offered me the job. I accepted. One of my first responsibilities was to find my replacement. Since I had expected this to happen at some point, I had given this some thought. In the time that I had been in LA, I had developed a relationship with one of the claim representatives, a Japanese man in the LA claims department who handled workers compensation claims and had been with Aetna for several years. He worked with claims for several NAD accounts and had participated in claim reviews. I was always impressed with his knowledge and his ability to relate to people and thought he would be a valuable addition to NAD.

He had a very pessimistic view of his career opportunities with Aetna and I wasn't sure he would warm to this move or that I could get the manager to go along with it. I knew it was somewhat unusual to put someone in that position without going through the customary selection process, but I thought it was worth the try. After all, I knew **you can get people to do almost anything if your motives are pure, your rationale convincing and sincere, and the discussion takes place in an atmosphere of trust and mutual respect.**

I broached the idea with him. At first he was very reluctant, but with some arm twisting and the assurance he would be working for me, he agreed if offered, to accept the job. I warned him it was not a done deal, because I had to convince the boss. He understood.

When I approached the boss, his initial reaction was negative. He knew my candidate, but not well. He insisted on going through the regular hiring process. I was persistent and said we have the perfect person right across the hall; why go through the expense and time of searching for someone else. I reiterated he knew the territory, knew most of our accounts and had great people skills. My experience with Hensel Phelps had highlighted the importance of relationships and I thought he would be great at it. Also, he had served his time in the claims department and deserved the opportunity to pursue something different. The boss was not convinced, but said he would think about it. My final comment was, he will be working for me and I will assume complete responsibility for his performance.

The next day, the boss agreed to extend the offer. We did and he accepted. I was ecstatic. In just seven years I had my first supervisory job. The five P's were delivering beyond my initial expectations. In a very short time, I had gone from having none to several major accounts.

Hensel Phelps' renewal was pretty much put to bed, so I could focus on getting to know the other accounts better and wrapping up the deal with Liebherr. This turned out to be a very interesting experience, dealing with Germans who knew little about the American legal system and were absolutely amazed to find they could be held liable in a product liability case if somebody miss-used one of their products and was injured. We worked through the issues, put together a competitive program and got the order. Another first for me.

With the program details in place, it was time to visit Liebherr's corporate offices in Norfolk, Virginia. I decided to take my new hire with me since I knew he was going to take over the handling of the account soon. He turned out to be an excellent choice. He was great with accounts, great with brokers and established some very strong relationships that proved critical to the retention of several accounts. He and I traveled a lot together. Seattle and San Francisco were almost weekly trips and Greely and Salt Lake City rounded out our agenda.

The meeting with Liebherr went well. We spent a lot of time talking about the American legal system, and the things they needed to do to mitigate their exposure. Our reputation in the construction industry gave them a lot of comfort. We wrapped things up and headed back to LA.

Since I knew "all work and no play, makes Johnny a dull boy", I really got into the recreational opportunities of Southern California. I also knew balance and renewal were important ingredients in maintaining my effectiveness. My boat arrived in January and I enjoyed launching it in Marina Del Rey and cruising the coastline. It was a gorgeous boat, loud and always attracted a lot of attention.

Our boss, with no warning resigned, to return to Dallas. We were shocked. His replacement had worked in the Houston

NAD office. Our office had grown considerably over the prior two years and, our administrative assistant was overworked. I approached our new boss about hiring another AA. He agreed and told me to find someone. We interviewed several candidates and finally hired Maria, a very pleasant, smart young lady from Czechoslovakia, who would report to me. In a very short time, we had diversified the LA office, one being Japanese, our new secretary, Czechoslovakian and me being Black, I was sure we had the most international team in the country. I was pleased.

In mid-1978, I got a call from Fred Rahn of Rahn & Company who handled the Sisters of Providence account. I had gotten to know Fred really well and we got along great. Fred was wealthy, a wine connoisseur and collector and loved sports cars. He said, "The next time you're in Seattle, I want to take you to dinner and discuss a proposition with you." As it turned out, I was going to be in Seattle in the next two days. We made a date for dinner.

Fred had reserved a private room at El Gaucho's, one of the finest restaurants in Seattle, with the most extensive wine cellar in the state. He ordered one of the most expensive bottles of wine I had ever seen, tasted it and sent it back, saying, it was not good. They brought another, all without ever questioning what was wrong. Fred was a regular customer, and I'm sure they understood he knew more about wine than most people at the restaurant. He had an eighteen hundred square foot wine cellar in the basement of his house. The new bottle came, Fred approved and we ordered dinner. Fred started by telling me what a great job I was doing on the Sisters of Providence account and how much they enjoyed working with me. He then offered me a job in his agency. He would double my salary, give me the opportunity to earn equity in the agency and move me to Seattle. I told him it was a very generous offer and I would think about it and let him know. The wine was incredible and the meal just as good. I had eaten at El Gaucho's before, but never with an eight hundred dollar bottle of wine.

The next day, I had meetings with Westin International and Morrison Knudsen Construction Company. Then I headed back to LA. On the flight back, I thought about Fred's offer. Equity in the agency would almost insure me being a millionaire in a short period of time. The agency was very successful and had a lock on several accounts that created a constant stream of income. So from a financial standpoint, this was a no brainer. The problem was financial security was only one part of my goal; I wanted to be a great leader, and I didn't think working with Fred would give me the opportunity to do that. After a discussion with my wife, I declined Fred's offer.

In October, 1978, my mother took her first plane ride. She, my sister Joyce and her husband Earl flew to LA. I was excited to have my family visit and planned an exciting agenda, including all of the major attractions. We went to Disneyland where my mother was overwhelmed with the flowers, Tijuana, where my sister got a kick out of negotiating with the vendors and the San Diego Zoo. The highlight, however, was a private guided tour of Universal Studios. The risk manager was delighted to show my family around and arranged for them to attend the filming of Sha Na Na, a TV show. It was an action-packed few days. Unfortunately, at the end of the week, my mother got a call from Chicago. My Uncle James had passed away from a heart attack. We were devastated, and my mother left immediately to be with his wife in Chicago. I would follow the next day. Uncle James was a big part of my life and I knew I was going to miss him.

From the day our new boss arrived in the office, he questioned why we were located in Los Angeles when most of our business was in Seattle, San Francisco and Denver. He also hated Los Angeles and loved San Francisco. He immediately started pushing to have the office moved. He wanted an office in San Francisco with a sub-office in Seattle. After lengthy negotiations, the home office agreed. He would be the manager of the main office in San Francisco, with a sub office in Seattle, run by an assistant manager reporting to him. Each office would have a full team, with the appropriate amount of administrative support. The assistant manager's job would be the only one of its kind in NAD.

The Seattle office would open in 1979 and handle, Washington, Oregon, Nevada, Idaho and Colorado. Since Seattle was considered a great place to live and the office would be responsible for some of Aetna's largest accounts, there was a lot of interest in the assistant manager position. Given his long tenure with Aetna, I thought the loss control supervisor would be the natural choice.

The manager of our St. Louis office had announced his retirement around the same time. I approached the boss with the perfect solution. Since the loss control supervisor had relationship issues with some of the accounts that Seattle would handle, I thought a fresh start for him in St. Louis was just what he needed. Given my relationship with the accounts and with his close guidance, I told him Seattle would be perfect for my first management job. He liked the idea, but wasn't sure he could sell Home office. I told him if he could sell moving the office to San Francisco with a sub in Seattle, this would be a piece of cake. I also knew the head of NAD in the home office was very pleased with my performance and had become a big supporter, so I thought this would be an easy sell for him.

I was going to be the manager of the Seattle sub-office! The loss control supervisor would go to Seattle for two months to help me set up the office and then he would move to St. Louis. I was beyond excited! I immediately went to work on planning the office. I knew the importance of the support work provided by the administrative staff and was not looking forward to finding someone locally that could handle the job. Our administrative assistant was a single parent with a six year old daughter, who was looking for a change and interested in moving to Seattle. The problem was Aetna didn't transfer administrative employees. I approached the boss about her transfer, but he felt he had used all his influence to get to where we were and was not willing to take this on. I asked him if it was okay with him if I tried.

My boss knew I had a good relationship with the head of NAD in Hartford and was willing to let me try to persuade him. After all, **I knew you could get people to do almost anything if your motives were pure, your rationale convincing and sincere, and the discussion takes place in an atmosphere of trust and mutual respect**. I called him and explained to him the many benefits of having an experienced administrative assistant on staff the day we opened in Seattle and, that she was very familiar with all of the accounts, had done a great job, was well- respected by the brokers and the accounts, and I thought would send a powerful message we were committed to maintaining superior service levels during this transition. I was told Aetna didn't transfer administrative employees. I reminded him the Seattle office would be the first expansion office for NAD, and I would think he would want to do everything possible to make sure it went smoothly. After a long discussion, he agreed to give her the full company transfer program to move to Seattle. My first Seattle employee was in place, and I was glad I wouldn't have to be concerned about that aspect of the new operation.

My wife did not want to move to Seattle, so we had the discussion that I think we both knew was inevitable. This was not what she signed up for. She had had three jobs since college and would have to get another. We also knew this was going to be a way of life for some time, and she was not prepared to do that. We decided to get a divorce. When I moved to Seattle, she would move back to New Jersey to be with her sister. We agreed she would take the car and I would take the furniture. It was an amicable separation and we remained friends for years afterward. A mutual friend flew out to LA to help her drive back to New Jersey and I started packing for Seattle.

When the announcement went out about the new office, the feedback was tremendously positive. We had a lot of business in Seattle and the prospect of having a local office was very appealing to the accounts and the brokers. I couldn't wait to form my new team and take on the challenges I knew we would face. My friend, Fred Rahn, called to offer his assistance in helping me get settled in Seattle. I also received calls from all the accounts and the brokers welcoming us to the city. I had a good feeling right from the start. This was going to be great! The movers arrived, and I arranged to have my boat shipped. I was off to The Great Northwest!

BECOMING
A LEADER

    The move to Seattle went extremely well. I found a first floor two-bedroom unit in a great high-rise condo in the Seward Park section of the city located at the south end of Lake Washington with a fabulous view of the lake and Mt. Rainier. It had a wrap-around balcony that extended out over the water. It was the perfect bachelor pad.
    We started assembling the team as soon as the move was approved, so by the time we got to Seattle the only position we needed to fill was for a second administrative assistant. My team would consist of the account representative for underwriting in the Houston office, the account representative for claims in Philadelphia and, the account representative for loss control in Charlotte. They would all be promoted to account supervisors and moved to Seattle. I was very pleased with my team. They were young, smart, ambitious, malleable, and eager to set the world on fire. Only thirty-one, I was the youngest NAD manager in the country, and had the youngest team. We were affectionately referred to as the "kids".
    The head of Johnson & Higgins, one of the country's largest brokerage firms and brokers for two of our largest accounts, Boeing and Westin International Hotels, concerned by the youthfulness of the team, wrote to the NAD home office questioning our apparent lack of experience. Two people who worked there and handled Boeing and Westin International, quickly came to my defense, stating they had the utmost

confidence in my ability to manage the office and trusted my judgment in the selection of the other team members. They also felt they had excellent administrative support. Reassured by his staff, this person would become one of our biggest supporters, but he should have communicated with his own people before writing to Hartford. My administrative assistant found someone from Seattle to fill the vacancy and we were fully staffed.

With some help from the San Francisco office, I and my staff worked on getting up to speed on our accounts as soon as possible. After several meetings, we decided, in addition to specific account assignments, everyone knowing more about all the accounts would insure continuity in service levels that would become the hallmark of our office. I had learned earlier that smart ambitious people have a large capacity for taking on meaningful responsibilities and always rise to the occasion. With such a young team (they were all in their twenties) I wanted to make sure there was as much back-up in the process as possible. We hit the ground running. The enthusiasm in the group was electrifying and I was reminded of E. M. Forster's quote; **"One person with passion is better than forty people merely interested"**. If that were true, and I had no doubt it was, with five passionate people, our success was guaranteed.

With my first management/ leadership position in place, it was time to formalize the skills I needed to perfect my leadership ability. I had continued to read about and observe leaders in action over the time I was with Aetna, and felt I had learned a lot. The five P's would always be the foundation for success, but leadership would require certain characteristics beyond the fundamentals. So I set about developing the traits that, when super-imposed on the five P's, would result in great leadership.

The Four Traits Critical For Great Leaders

1. **VISION** – A Japanese Proverb says: **"Vision without action is a daydream. Action without vision is a nightmare"**. Leaders have the ability to see the impossible, to not only look down the road, but around the corner. They can not only paint a picture of an inspired

future, they can get people to see that future and channel their energies into achieving it. Toba Beta said: **"Visionaries build what dreamers imagine"**. An effective vision creates the context and framework for all of the decisions made and activities undertaken in the entire organization. It is the filter through which all new ideas must pass. It is the catalyst for the innovation and creativity necessary for the continued progress of the organization. It is the inspiration, the motivation that drives people to achieve great things. It sustains the level of enthusiasm that is critical for all high-performing organizations. As Ralph Waldo Emerson said; **"Nothing great has ever been accomplished without enthusiasm"**.

2. <u>COURAGE</u> – Karl von Clausewitz said: **"Never forget no leader has ever become great without audacity"**. Great leaders must believe the impossible is doable, brave enough to trust in the abilities of his people and secure enough to encourage risk taking at every level of the organization. Once a shared vision is launched, the leader's role is to provide cover and fend off external and internal threats; to stand up to forces that could derail the dream.

3. <u>COMMUNICATION SKILLS</u> –Dale Carnegie said: **"When dealing with people, remember you are not dealing with creatures of logic, but creatures of emotion"**. In all my years in business I have found one of the biggest issues leaders have is the inability to tap into the emotions of the people they lead. Effective communications is the way. We all know orators that have been able to move the masses with the spoken word. Be it Patrick Henry's **"give me liberty or give me death"** or Martin Luther King's **"I Have A Dream"** or John F. Kennedy's **" Ask not what your country can do for you, but what you can do for your country"**, we've all been moved by the rhetoric of great leaders. To be able to

inspire people with an animated, from the heart speech, without the use of a teleprompter is a powerful tool. I have always believed it is difficult, if not impossible to inspire and motivate people, if you have to read what you're saying. If you don't believe what you're saying enough to be able to talk about it without an aid, it is highly unlikely you'll be able to convince anyone else. Additionally, great speakers tailor their speech to the reaction of the audience, which is difficult to do when you are reading. Experts say when listening to a speech, people remember the beginning and the end. Great speakers are **MASTERS OF THE MIDDLE**, and can compel the attention of the audience throughout the speech.

4. **VULNERABILITY**– This always evokes a violent reaction from people, since vulnerability is generally associated with weakness. Just the opposite is true. Eric Micha'el Leventhal said: **"We are at our most powerful the moment we no longer need to be powerful"**. Vulnerable leaders are strong and courageous, willing to acknowledge they don't have the answers and need their followers to develop the solutions. In other words, they are comfortable with their limitations. I know of no more an effective way to get **Employee Engagement** than appealing for help in running the business and achieving the mission of the organization. The people you lead know you don't have all the answers, don't expect you to, and consider it dishonest when you try to pretend. A, "We're all in this together", approach will create a sense of ownership among employees that will generate the discretionary effort necessary for successful companies to operate, continuously outperform the competition and keep their customers begging for more.

    I felt good about the traits I had identified and knew they were consistent with my views of what leadership should be. They were also consistent with Theory Y and would allow for the harnessing of the collective genius of all employees necessary for the creation of a high performing organization.

My team started to jell right away. Since we, except for our local hire, were all transplants, we became like a little family and spent many social hours together having dinner, skiing, or just hanging out. Night skiing was very popular in Seattle and two or three times a week we would leave work, head to the slopes, ski for a couple of hours and be home in bed by midnight. This gave us a lot of time to collaborate on what was happening with our accounts and keep everyone up to date on the latest issues or opportunities. Since we all loved what we were doing, this was never a burden and often resulted in some creative ideas on how to conduct business. For instance, one night at dinner our administrative assistant suggested we should learn the birthdays of all risk managers, arrange a conference call that day, and sing happy birthday. It sounds like a small thing on the surface, but it was a huge hit and I'm sure made a lot of business meetings easier.

As a new bachelor, my social life was in high gear. Shortly after arriving in Seattle, I decided to go to one of the local hot spots. In checking out the crowd I noticed a lady that had a striking resemblance to Diana Ross and was being harassed by two soldiers. Since I could tell she wanted to be rescued, I asked her to dance. She agreed and we spent the rest of the night together. A few years older than I, a divorcee with two children, she worked for the mayor and was a prominent member of the Seattle social scene. She took me to Henry's Off Broadway, a restaurant and bar in town, the after-work hangout for the young, up and coming executives in the city. She introduced me to the Henry's gang and we spent many hours there.

Shortly after meeting her, she said if she was going to be seen around town with me, I had to upgrade my dress to something more appropriate for a young executive. I was more of a trendy dresser than a business dresser. She took me to Nordstrom's and introduced me to a friend who was a salesman in the men's department. I bought three suits, several shirts and several ties. I never dressed the same again.

Interestingly, with all of my planning, I never really considered how I dressed. I would discover that it is a big part of how you are perceived. We have all heard the saying, "you only get one chance to make a first impression." Your dress is a big part of that. Being a quick learner I soon went from shopping at Nordstrom's to having my suits and shirts tailor made. Over the coming years, I gained the reputation as one of the best-dressed executives at Aetna.

Around the same time, my good friend, Fred Rahn, decided I needed to upgrade my transportation since I was still driving a company car. He owned three Ferraris and two Porsches but was not offering either for my use. He took me to see one of his friends in the business and explained I needed an affordable, but nice, sports car befitting my young-executive status. Fred was kind of an expert when it came to sports cars, so I knew I was in good hands. After a lot of discussion about several options, we decided on an Alfa Romeo Spider convertible. I chose a chocolate brown with Carmel interior. It was gorgeous!

The team was in high gear. Even though they were some of the largest and most complex Aetna wrote, we had very few issues with our accounts. I attribute that to the effectiveness of the team. We did a lot of traveling and entertaining to make sure our relationships were always strong. I also made several trips back to the home office, mostly client trips, and always made it a point to touch base with Ollie. The debate over Theory X vs Theory Y was more intense than ever, and I made sure I was a part of the conversation. We also had several home office people visit Seattle, including the head of NAD, who came out for the 1980 Boeing Renewal. The Boeing renewal went well and the account and broker shared with him how pleased they were with the service provided by "the kids". He was pleased and headed back to Hartford, knowing that the Seattle NAD office was in good hands.

Insurance is a cyclical business driven mainly by interest rates and the availability of investment income. Because insurance companies handle a lot of money, the opportunity for investment income is huge, particularly when interest rates are high and investment risk low. In a soft market, companies will cut the rates they charge customers, attract more customers and invest the additional premium income. The theory is what they lose on the underwriting side can be more than offset by the increase in investment income. This frequently starts a pricing war with rates falling lower and lower, which is good for customers, but makes it difficult for companies to hold on to their clients. 1980 was a soft market and NAD lost several accounts countrywide. The Seattle office was the only office in the country that didn't lose a single account. Kudos to the Kids!

I was very proud of the way my team had developed and the impressive results we were producing. It was obvious that we had selected some good people and were doing a lot of the right things. I combined this with my leadership studies to identify the six critical characteristics **of High Performing Organizations.**

The Six Critical Characteristics Of High Performing Organizations

1. **TRUST-** While it is difficult to say one characteristic is more important than the others trust is very high on the priority list, mainly because it provides the foundation for most of the others. It is not an overstatement to say that you will never create a high-performing organization without it. I have often compared the level of trust necessary in high-performing organizations to that which exists between two mountain climbers who must trust that their partner has properly hammered the pitons to which they attach a climbing rope, often the only thing between them and a fatal fall. The good news for leaders, as I learned as a student at Hampton, trust is a given, so unless you do something to create distrust, the organization will assume you are trustworthy. That being said, I have always been amazed at how quickly and thoughtlessly would-be

leaders destroy trust and then wonder why performance suffers. Then they spend countless resources in a fruitless effort to try to restore it.

2. **CANDOR** – I have never understood people who make bad, costly decisions and don't want to be told about them. How arrogant do you have to be to think that you could not benefit from the wisdom of people around you, when in most cases, they have more information about the subject than you? To create an environment where people are fearful of speaking out about problems or opportunities is to stifle the growth of the organization and jeopardize its future. Jack Welch of GE called a lack of candor the "biggest dirty little secret in business". A healthy environment is where people not only feel free to speak out, but see it as an **obligation.** If your idea of candor is a suggestion box in a corner of the cafeteria or an anonymous email drop, you've completely missed the point. Organizations with a high degree of trust have no need for anonymity.

3. **TEAMWORK** – Tom Wilson said: **"Many of us are more capable than some of us…but none of us is as capable as all of us!!"** Working together is an absolute must in high-performing organizations. Having a compelling Vision and an honorable mission are useless without the teamwork necessary to implement the plan. Collaboration among team members is critical to the efficient operation of the team and must occur in a trusting environment where candor is expected.

4. **DIVERSITY** – This has been one of the most misunderstood concepts in business over the last fifty years. Diversity initiatives have been so mired in issues of **Race** and **Gender,** that its true meaning and purpose has been lost. If companies truly understood diversity, why would you ever need to put someone in charge of it? If leaders truly understood the origin of innovation and creativity why wouldn't diversity be the number one priority on every leader's list? Diversity is all about

perspective. Race and gender offer a different perspective, but so does the college you attended, the section of the country you're from, whether you're right-brained or left, your economic background, your age and many other conditions. This kind of diversity drives new product development, improved customer service and a fully engaged workforce. Different perspectives result in different points of view, which in a trusting environment should generate a healthy debate, creative solutions to problems, and innovative approaches to new ideas. James Surowiecki said: **"Diversity and independence are important because the best collective decisions are the product of disagreement and contest, not consensus or compromise"**. Great leaders recognize while it's desirable to surround yourself with people with complementary skills, when it comes to perspective, you also want contradictory views.

5. **EMPOWERMENT** -Empowerment is one of the key ingredients in a high-performing organization. Efficient organizations make sure decisions are made at the proper level of the organization, so the CEO is not making decisions that should be made by the front-line staff, and the front-line staff has the authority to make decisions crucial to customer satisfaction. Contrary to popular belief, empowerment does not mean everybody is involved in every decision, just those appropriate for a given position.

6. **ACCOUNTABILITY**–Winston Churchill said: **"It is not enough that we do our best; sometimes we must do what is required"**. This is often one of the hardest characteristics for leaders to practice. You cannot implement the above five and not hold people accountable for their actions and performance. When you fail to hold people accountable you penalize the organization twice, first with the fall-off of the performance of the guilty employee and second with the negative impact on morale for the rest of the team. The leader selects good people, trains them, gives them the support they need to get the job done and then holds them

accountable for results. Anything less is detrimental to the team.

I was very confident these were the right characteristics since I was living them every day with my team and could see up close and personal how effective they were. The Seattle job proved to be the perfect first management job for me. It gave me the opportunity to test Theory Y in a real-world setting with a team small enough to respond to quickly in the event an adjustment was necessary.

Seattle is a great city and I was enjoying every bit of it. Bachelor life suited me well and my team was knocking it out of the park every day. As the saying goes, "all good things must come to an end", and in early 1981 I got a call from the head of NAD offering me a job in the home office. I had been in Seattle just over a year, and was not expecting this. His manager of claim administration had been promoted and he needed a replacement. A home office staff position would make me an officer of the company, which meant I could sign official documents on behalf of the company and my name would appear in some SEC filings. I would have one assistant and share a secretary with my boss, the director. Naturally, he stressed what an honor this was and that the home office experience would be good for my long-term career aspirations.

With mixed emotions I accepted the home office job. Seattle, although a short stay, was an unbelievable blast. I was going to miss the team and I think they all knew our experience together had been unique and not likely to continue with my replacement. My leaving was difficult for us all but everybody understood it was necessary.

I decided to drive back east so I invited my brother Mason to spend a few days with me and then we would drive back. It was a good opportunity for me to spend some quality time with him; we hadn't seen much of each other since I left Richmond. We planned to drive to Denver, spend the night with a friend and then drive the rest of the way, non-stop. Mother-nature had other plans. The Denver leg went as planned, but we awoke the next morning to a blizzard. We drove off anyway and made it to Hays Kansas before they closed the highway. We spent the night in

Hays, and the next day drove non-stop to Richmond. It was a good trip and I enjoyed the time with my brother.

I spent two days in Richmond visiting the family and then headed to Hartford. I was excited about the new job. Working in the home office would round out my experience and, give me much needed insight into the support they provided. I also would be a stone's throw away from Ollie's office. The big question was, were they **ready for my brand of leadership?**

AH, THE
HOME OFFICE

Because of my many visits, I was very familiar with Hartford. As a bachelor, I decided I wanted to live downtown, to be close to the action. I found a nice two bedroom loft apartment in a renovated department store right on Main St. I think I was the only Aetna officer who lived downtown in an apartment. My peers were all married with two kids, a station wagon and lived in the suburbs. Since I was comfortable in being different, this was of little concern to me but was noticed by others and created constant chatter. Shortly after I arrived I was approached by a senior officer and asked if I had any plans to get married. I promptly replied, no.

As an officer I got a padded cubicle with a wooden desk and a leather chair with two side chairs. I found out early these symbols were a very big part of the home office culture and people could tell your position in the hierarchy just by the size of your cubicle and your desk. I thought them a strange breed these home office people. I also got an assigned space in the enclosed officers' parking garage and could eat in the officers' dining room where there was table-serve as opposed to cafeteria style. I had arrived!

Most big companies distinguish between home office employees and those who work in the field. It generally revolves around the home office being overhead, out of touch with reality and more of an obstacle to performance than a help, while the field generates the revenue, knows what the customers want, but is seldom consulted. This creates a tension that is sometimes healthy, but more often disrupts the smooth operation of the company. The most successful field offices ignore directives from home office when they have no application and make the decisions appropriate to the local operation. This came with some risks, but the strong field leaders knew the benefits were greater. That being said, the home office did play a very valuable role in the support of the field offices' operations. That support includes new product development, technology improvements, regulatory compliance, brand protection, continuity, human resource support and training.

My new boss was very conservative, by the book and had reached his plateau. Our secretary was a delightful young lady, who right from the start intended to find me a suitable wife. My assistant was energetic, smart, ambitious, outspoken, creative and looking to propel her career to the next level. My new responsibilities entailed working with the NAD teams on claim issues, designing special claim handling procedures for accounts, providing a liaison with the claims department and resolving issues with individual claims. I would travel to various renewal meetings when claims was a central problem. It provided me with the opportunity to broaden my knowledge of the businesses NAD handled and my west coast experience proved valuable in several claim situations.

One advantage of being in the home office was the close proximity to training. Shortly after I arrived I attended a week-long management training seminar for new managers that mainly focused on the mechanics of the job, the performance management process, development planning, and salary administration. I found it helpful, but not career changing. I also attended a three-day ethics course at the University of Hartford where we discussed the importance of honesty, trustworthiness, reliability and safe guarding the public trust. It stressed keeping your promises and obeying the law. I found myself wondering why the people in the class weren't taught these things by their mothers. I guess I was lucky.

The head of NAD conducted my first home office performance review which was a little unusual since it was normally handled by your immediate boss. It was a very good review culminating with him telling me I would be put on the company's **High Potential List**. This was huge, since it identified middle-level managers considered potential vice-presidents and entitled them to a different level of training opportunities. The crown jewel of this was a six-weeks training course at Fairfield University, where the leading experts in different fields were brought in to conduct the sessions. The selected twelve to fifteen candidates would live in designated quarters on campus during the course, eating, studying and playing with their colleagues, with no trips home. I was sure this would provide some meaningful training and the opportunity to rub elbows with the competition. It would go a long way providing the preparation necessary for me to become a great leader.

My daily responsibilities became routine, even boring. I missed the action from being in the field and soon I realized that being away from the front line was not where I wanted to be. Then I got a call from the manager of our Chicago office about a very large account that was in danger. We insured one of the largest home protective systems manufacturers and installers (fire and burglar alarms) in the country. One of their customers had suffered a fire loss, claimed a defect in the fire alarm system and our claims department had settled the claim paying the homeowner over $100,000. However, the contract between the manufacturer and the homeowner limited the liability of the manufacturer to five hundred dollars. This clause had been in existence for well over fifty years, had withstood numerous court challenges and was the backbone of the industry. Without the protection of this clause our insured would have to exit the business and was planning to move their account from us and file a lawsuit. The manager wanted me to come out and help him save the account and prevent a costly lawsuit. In two weeks we would have our meeting.

This was what I lived for and immediately started my preparation. My goal was clear: I had to save the account and avoid the lawsuit. I contacted the claim department and got all of the information on the case. They had settled the loss on a compromise basis because they questioned whether the clause would hold up and felt the safest alternative was to compromise. They never considered the larger implication to the insured's business. My assistant and I spent days analyzing every case ever tried around this clause and the court's reasoning in each. I knew at a minimum I would have to go to the meeting and justify the position we took.

Our research revealed the client was right. The clause

had stood up against numerous challenges from several different directions. The courts had ruled not having this clause would put an enormous burden on manufacturers of these alarms and decided the public good would be best served with the clause intact. So my job was clear. I had to convince our insured settling this claim did not set a precedent and the integrity of the clause had not been compromised.

I headed to Milwaukee knowing more about the fire protective business than I ever imagined. The NAD manager and the broker picked me up at the airport and I could tell instantly they were not going to be helpful. The threat of the loss of such a large account had left them barely functional. We arrived at the account's corporate headquarters a few minutes before the meeting began in the boardroom and I was stunned at seeing the number of people waiting for me. Our host served coffee and donuts outside the meeting room before we started and we engaged in desultory small talk. All I could think of was how I could possibly accomplish my goals in the face of being severely outnumbered. The division president announced the start of the meeting and opened the doors to the boardroom. It was huge with a large mahogany table, with microphones at each seat and large leather chairs. Then I saw what I needed. At the head of the table was a chair larger than any others and raised about three inches off the floor, obviously where the chairman of the board sat. I was the first person in the room. I went straight to the head of the table and sat in the chairman's seat. There were some stares but no one said a word. The attendees at the meeting included the division president, his general counsel and two other division lawyers, the corporate senior vice president for that division, his general counsel and two other lawyers, the risk manager and his assistant, a secretary to take notes, five or six other people who just observed, the NAD manager, the broker and me. The division president opened the meeting, laid out the issues and the battle was on. The symbolism of the chairman's chair was amazing and had the effect I had hoped for: a receptive audience. No one in the room could attack the chair, so, when I spoke everyone listened.

We had a three-hour meeting that was as intense as any

I've ever attended. My position was our action in compromising the claim settlement hadn't set a precedent and the integrity of the clause was still intact. The only way a new precedent could be established was through another court case and we avoided that by settling the claim. I had numerous court cases to support my position and while none were directly on point, they were close enough to be convincing.

The meeting ended without a final decision, but I felt good about how things went. I was also completely exhausted and almost collapsed in the car. The broker, who had not uttered a single word during the meeting, was amazed I had single-handedly controlled that many high-level corporate officers. I told him it was the chair and he got a kick out of hearing that was a deliberate move on my part. The NAD manager rattled on about having never seen such a performance and if we lost the account it wouldn't be for lack of trying. He also felt at the very least we had avoided a lawsuit.

When I got back in the office I shared the experience with my bosses. They too enjoyed the part about the chair. Two days later we got the word. The account was staying with Aetna, and no lawsuit would be forthcoming on the condition we wouldn't settle another similar claim without the account's agreement. We agreed. I had hit another home run. This time I hadn't asked for the tough assignment, but the effect was the same. It also reaffirmed **that you can get people to do almost anything if your motives are pure, your rationale convincing and sincere and the discussions take place in an atmosphere of trust and mutual respect.**

My secretary was serious about finding me a wife, even though I wasn't looking for one, and one day after attending a career development workshop, rushed into my office and announced she had found the perfect person. The facilitator for the workshop, a rising star and team leader for one of the benefit units was tall, attractive, smart and most important, not wearing a wedding band. I thanked my secretary and assured her I was fine and not anxious to engage in a serious relationship.

The very next week I was attending a social function at

the Sheraton Hotel in downtown when I saw the facilitator. I introduced myself and told her the story about my secretary. She said it was the weakest pick up line she had ever heard. I assured her it was a true story but she was not convinced. However, she was interested enough to have lunch with me the following day. An Aetna lifer, divorced with two children in high school, she was several years older than I but didn't look it. We began a lengthy relationship and she later would play a critical role in one of my most ambitious undertakings. My secretary was pleased.

    I continued to have an occasional lunch with Ollie and our discussions on leadership grew more and more intense. He was not a Theory Y convert, but did feel changes in Aetna's stated management philosophy were needed. The company hired the best and brightest from the best business schools, but turnover after three or four years was too high. I impressed on him you couldn't hire smart people, lock them in a box, tell them what to do and how to do it and expect them to be happy. Bright ambitious employees wanted to be full partners in running the business and reaping the rewards of its success. The company had started to incorporate the principles of decentralized management into its training but there was a sense it was an intellectual exercise with no real commitment to its implementation. Ollie asked several times why I was so committed to the concept. I shared with him my experience growing up on the farm and my Seattle experience, with which he was familiar. Additionally, I told him it was the natural order. Given a clear vision, a defined mission and a comprehensive strategic plan, people can and will figure out how to execute it and are willing to be held accountable for the results. He was not convinced, but I could tell he was wavering.

    My much anticipated training session at Fairfield University finally arrived. We got a list of attendees and I was surprised to see only two of the fifteen people attending had field experience. I thought the selection process was lacking and worried it reflected an out-of-touch home office that had little appreciation for what happened in the field. We also got numerous reading materials and had to complete a three-sixty performance evaluation before we arrived. This is a comprehensive review, conducted by an outside party that includes feedback from peers, bosses, subordinates and customers. I could tell this was going to be serious business and I could hardly wait.

We spent the first few days reviewing our three-sixty evaluations and going through the Myers Briggs personality typing exercise. I found Myers Briggs fascinating. While some of it was instinctive, strategies to deal with the various personality types provided some very useful information. My score on intuition intrigued the group and the instructor said it was the highest he had ever seen for a male and rivaled the highest he had seen for females. I told him it was probably because I grew up in a household with seven strong women that had a significant influence on my life philosophies and how I viewed the world. He gave a rather emotional lecture on the power of intuition if you have the courage to trust it. I agreed.

The days at Fairfield were long and filled with learning. We had some evening sessions, but most nights were spent hanging out in the lobby playing cards or Pong and Packman. This was a very competitive group and even the games took on an air of ferocity. Fortunately there were no fistfights. The courses covered everything and stressed strategic and operational planning and execution. We spent hours debating the Japanese vs the American approach and reviewed several case studies of each. We discussed Theory X and Theory Y and the group was equally divided in its support. Theory Xer's dismissed Japanese superior productivity and quality as an anomaly. Centralized vs decentralized management styles also occupied days of discussion with ample case studies. I was very impressed with our instructors, who facilitated the discussions/debates without overly influencing them. They were dealing with Aetna's best and brightest and their job was to nurture the talent that was already there.

Most of my colleagues had attended Ivy League schools; several had MBAs. However, I saw in them a lack of common sense, a skewed world view that ignored reality, and an unhealthy disdain for people who were not like them.

One day we debated the difference between being right and being effective. I argued that when you are leading people the key is to be effective. If you're right but can't convince your followers, then all is lost. Your job as leader is not to be right, but to elicit the right answers/solutions from your employees. The Theory X's felt it was unnecessary to convince people to do something when all you had to do was tell them and then hold them accountable if they failed to comply. I was feeling better about my chances with each passing day!

Dr. Bob Mitchell was scheduled to give us a motivational speech on the morning of the last day, and we all thought he had drawn the short straw. Giving a motivational speech to fifteen hyped up executives that had been cooped up at Fairfield University for six weeks had to be daunting. When Dr. Bob arrived the evening before and didn't dine with the group as all other instructors had, we were prepared to crucify him the next morning. We spent the evening discussing his arrogance.

The morning arrived and unlike the other instructors, Dr. Bob had a formal introduction that included his resume. He entered the amphitheater from the back, walked directly on stage, and without a single note started to speak. He was dressed like he stepped off the cover of Esquire Magazine and spoke in a tone that demanded attention. We all sat up a little straighter in our seats and for the next two hours were transfixed as Dr. Bob talked to us about leadership, confidence, self-esteem, passion emotion and the absolute necessity of loving what you do. He walked back and forth across the stage and when he finished I thought he had to be exhausted. We gave him a standing ovation! It is one of the most powerful speeches I've heard and re-enforced my belief in the power of tapping into the emotions of people. Dr. Bob had **Mastered the Middle!**

Fairfield was exhausting but packed with information. I could see why it was the crown jewel of the leadership training program and thought it a shame it was reserved for such a limited few.

The next few weeks were uneventful and I found myself yearning for the field. I had been in the home office for just a year but knew I wanted to be back in the field. Then, one day, Ollie walked into my office, plopped into one of my side chairs and said

"Al, how would you like to put your leadership philosophy to the test?" I said, "Hey, I'm always up for a challenge", but I wasn't prepared for what came next. He told me the Commercial Insurance Department Manager in New York City had just been promoted to General Manager and I would replace him. The CID manager, as they were known, was responsible for underwriting, loss control policy processing and premium audit. From New York City, the largest and most complex office in the country, it was a sure path to general manager. It was a huge promotion, with a significant raise, and regarded as one of the toughest jobs in the company. After I recovered from the shock, I replied with all the confidence I could muster, I absolutely wanted it. I did caution him my generalist training hadn't included any time in underwriting. He said, "I don't want you to be an underwriter, I want you to be a leader". Then he said, "It's done and we'll work out the transition details later," and he left.

I was trying to figure out the implications of what had just happened. First, to have the offer come from Ollie, the head of the division and not my immediate boss was highly unusual. Second, to conduct an experiment like this in arguably the toughest market in the country was risky and out of character for a conservative company like Aetna that was still debating its future leadership philosophy. And finally, failure in this office could be catastrophic given the high visibility of New York and the constant scrutiny of the industry on everything that happens there. This was my toughest assignment yet and although I didn't ask for it, I couldn't wait to get started. Not only was I going back to the field, but this was my re-entry into the mainstream. I wondered if this would have happened if I hadn't walked into Ollie's office during my orientation visit to the home office back in 1975.

After just a year I was leaving the home office and the people I had gotten to know there. This was always the hard part for me. The emotional attachment to the people was always difficult for me to handle. My assistant arranged my going away party and it was pretty well attended. I think curiosity was a big factor. Just like my arrival in Newark as the only person to accept a lateral transfer there, people wanted to see the person who would accept the CID job in New York City with no underwriting background or training. As one of my parting gifts, my assistant wrote the following poem:

>Al Austin joined Aetna in Claim,
>From Richmond to Hartford he came.
>3 stops on the way,
>10 years the delay,
>Now he's off to New York to find fame.
>
>What New York doesn't know we will state
>'Bout his bets and his slow walkin gait.
>They had better prepare
>For his droopy eyed stare,
>In the mornings when he shows up late.
>
>The beard and mustache give him style.
>He's made friends everywhere with his smile.
>The women all wait,
>Their names he keeps straight,
>While remaining calm all the while.
>
>For this class jump you've got to be glad
>Cuz you'll pay for that Manhattan pad,
>Though we know you must go,
>We just want you to know,
>You'll always be missed here in NAD!

Immortalized in a poem; it doesn't get any better than that!

The poem was widely distributed!

It was 1982. I was moving for the fifth time in eight years and loving every minute of it.

The movers came, I packed the Alfa Romeo and prepared for the short drive down Interstate 95 to my new home in the **Big Apple!**

THE BIG APPLE EXPERIMENT

I was very familiar with the City since I visited several times after moving to Hartford. I knew I didn't want to live in Manhattan, but close enough to take full advantage of its nightlife and have a convenient commute, so I decided to live in New Jersey. I found a lovely seventh floor, two-bedroom condo in Edgewater, New Jersey, right on the Hudson River, with a fantastic view of the City. It was a short ten minute drive south to Hoboken where I could take the PATH train into the World Trade Center, have a short walk to my office in the financial district on William Street, and be at my desk in thirty minutes. It was perfect.

Before I left Hartford, Ollie warned me my reception in New York wouldn't be a warm one. The General Manager vehemently opposed my being put in the CID manager's position. Since general managers usually have a lot to say about their staff, he felt I was being forced on him and he was right. He thought someone without an underwriting background and from National Accounts couldn't possibly run the largest CID department in the company in the most complex market.

The GM had his own story. He started with Aetna in the mail room in New York and was now the general manager. He was set to retire in two years after more than forty years with the company, and thought I would endanger his legacy. In my first meeting with him he was very open about his feelings, stating he heard I was a nice guy and was sorry that I was being put in such an impossible position, because I had no chance of succeeding. He vowed to do everything he could to help me but held little hope that would be enough. I assured him I had the utmost confidence, I could not only handle the job, but was likely to be the best CID manager in the company and with his help, I couldn't miss. He wished me luck. I liked him.

Being back in the main stream meant a return to the

world of the law of large numbers. Unlike NAD, the standard commercial operation was true insurance. As the CID manager I was responsible for underwriting, policy processing, loss control and premium audit. The 175 people in my department included four underwriting unit managers, a processing manager, a premium audit manager and a loss control manager. The biggest difference between NAD and standard commercial was the size of accounts and the number of agents we dealt with. In NAD we dealt with a small number of agents and accounts, where in standard commercial we had a large number of agents and thousands of accounts. We did business through independent agents who represented many companies seeking the best deal for their clients. Since most of the accounts were small, Main-street type accounts, the margins on any individual account were very small. Therefore, we managed our relationship with the agents on a book-of-business basis, meaning we were more concerned about the profitability of the agent's total book of business with us than any individual account.

Aetna's strength was dealing with loyal agents who received a lot of support from the company and were prone to favor us over other companies in their agency. New York was not that kind of market. New York agents had no loyalty, didn't need Aetna's support and were basically price driven. The market was also dominated by the large brokers where, in most cases, we had no relationship. As a result, the office had difficulty growing revenue. We had to be competitive and win accounts on merit alone.

The underwriters worked with an assigned group of agents to select and price the accounts they thought would give us the best opportunity to make money. Since we had to compete with the other companies in the agent's office, we had to negotiate account premiums. Larger accounts, usually over $100,000, required the expertise of a home office referral unit, which resulted in tension between the home office and the field over who controlled the underwriting and pricing decisions for these accounts. Absent written rules, it usually came down to the strength of the field management team and their willingness to take responsibility for the results.

To select the highest quality accounts, underwriters need the input of the loss control department and actuaries. The loss control staff conducts onsite inspections, reports their findings to underwriting and recommends safety improvements to the insured. Actuaries supply a rate to arrive at a premium that best represents an account's potential exposure. For instance, the revenue a florist generates from flower sales would be the best indicator of activity in the store and thus exposure to accidents. The underwriter would use sales numbers times the rate to develop the annual premium. Since premiums are developed on a prospective basis, the underwriters estimate sales for a given year to determine the premium. At the end of the year, when the books are closed, the premium audit department examines the books to get the actual sales figures and the premium is adjusted accordingly.

By far the processing manager had the toughest job in CID. Before technology transformed insurance and many other industries, we had ninety people who rated, typed and assembled the individual policies. The numerous opportunities for errors led to complaints from agents about the poor quality of our policies. The company's standard for error ratio was nine percent and New York was constantly at thirty-five to forty percent. The general manager considered this one of the biggest problems in the office. He yearned for the day we met the company standard and had a successful home office audit. It hadn't happened in years, if ever.

Despite the issues the office was borderline profitable. My job was to fix processing, grow revenue and maintain profitability.

My first staff meeting lasted a full day. The feedback on my staff was they were all solid citizens, but no super stars. The high cost of living and the competitive market made it difficult to get people to move to New York, so I thought solid citizens were pretty good. I laid out the issues as I saw them and a reasonable time frame for correcting them. The group's response caught me a little by surprise when they said, "That's the same things the last four CID managers have said, so what's going to be different this time"? I said, "I can't speak for the last four CID managers, but with 175 bright minds, and their creative ideas, plus unlimited resources and support from home office, if we can't figure out how to make New York work, we should all resign". After an awkward silence I told them that I didn't have a silver bullet or a magic wand, but I had unwavering confidence in people to accomplish great things. Then I said from this day forward each of you should consider it your responsibility to help fix what's wrong regardless of the area it's in, that we were in this together and would sink or swim as a team; that they could count on me to provide cover, buck the status quo and do whatever we thought was best for New York, even if it was contrary to some home office mandate. Then we had a lively discussion that lasted for hours. I thought they were knowledgeable, candid and passionate enough to pull this off. I would probably have to make some changes, but for the most part, I liked what I saw. The weakest member of the group was the processing manager, in that position for three years, and apparently burned out. I knew he would have to be replaced.

Shortly after I left home office, Ollie resigned. I knew he had issues with the CEO, but this was a surprise. I always wondered if he knew he was going to leave when he sent me to New York. He was a mentor and ally, and I was going to miss him.

To get to know our key agents and have their feedback on our performance, I asked each unit manager to give me a list of their top ten agents and the vital statistics on each. I also asked the marketing manager to give me his list of our top fifty agents. Managing the agency plant was the responsibility of marketing, but required a lot of collaboration with underwriting. With this list in hand, I set about arranging meetings with each agent, accompanied by the respective unit manager and sometimes, the marketing manager. One advantage of working in the city was that we could have five or six agents in the same building, so I planned to visit everyone on the list in three weeks.

I was also getting to know the people in the office. I had decided "management by wandering about" was going to be my style. I didn't want the information I got to be filtered through the management team and risk missing some critical input that could significantly affect our operation. This made the managers a little uncomfortable, but I was sure they would relax after they found out I was not doing this to create a "got-cha" moment, but to gather information that would allow us to make better decisions. I always preferred this method of monitoring to reading performance reports weeks after the events occurred. Real-time information is invaluable when you're in turn-around mode. I also could hear what the front-line staff thought and get their ideas about what we should be doing. I would often spend an hour sitting at an underwriter's desk discussing their latest encounter with the home office referral unit or an agent that was being uncooperative or something happening in processing that was making their job difficult, and sometimes a suggestion as to how we could make processing more effective. After several weeks of this, people would walk into my office and offer advice on a whole host of issues. This was exactly the kind of environment I was trying to create and it was working. Everybody was engaged and felt an obligation to do whatever they could to make the organization better.

    My agency visits provided the feedback I needed. In a nutshell, our service was bad, the quality of our policies was poor and our underwriters were more inclined to decline an account than try to write it. Their declination rate with us was significantly higher than any other company and, as a result, we were less likely to get their best accounts. Aetna was the premiere company in the P & C business and they would really like to see us get our act together.

    In my individual discussions with underwriters, I had detected a protective air I thought could be unhealthy. The last two home office audits were very bad and people decided it was safer to say no than risk getting criticized by some home office auditor, second guessing their decision. I asked each unit manager to give me the documentation for the last twenty declinations for his unit. When an agent wants us to write an account, they send in a submission which contains the information necessary for underwriting and pricing the account. A part of that information is the specifications for coverage and/or pricing approach, typically a list of fifteen to twenty items. My review revealed underwriters would look at the specifications and mark in red those we couldn't do or were questionable and if more than three, decline the account. Negotiations start with specifications which may be preferred but are not absolute. I thought roughly sixty percent of the declinations could have been written.

With this information and the feedback from the agents, I gathered the entire department together to share my findings and update them on what was going on. I would hold all employee meetings at least once a month. I told them about our efforts to improve processing, about my agency visits and what I learned and the results of my review of declinations. I reiterated our need to increase revenue. I then said, from this day forward, when a submission came in from an agent, we would review the specifications and place a green check mark beside everything we could do easily. Then, after discussion with another underwriter or the unit manager, unless the quality indicated a declination, we would identify items that might require negotiation and develop a plan to write the account. I then passed out green pens and promised them they wouldn't have to fear being second-guessed by home office ever again as long as they exercised good judgment. I would protect them and I was more than capable of doing it.

Shortly after this meeting the processing manager resigned. I had asked him for a plan to turn his department around and to identify additional resources to help him. He said he didn't think he could live up to my expectations and wanted to save me the trauma of having to fire him. I thanked him for his service to Aetna, for his consideration of me and told him I thought he had made the right decision.

Before the ink was dry on the resignation, one of the underwriting unit managers was in my office. He asked for the processing job, and told me he was sure he could get the results I wanted. I asked him why he was so sure. He said being in underwriting and on the receiving end of a lot of the problems he was very familiar with the issues and felt with the proper leadership the department could be turned around. He knew there were some very capable people in the department that just needed the right motivation and support to right the ship. I told him I admired his **proactivity** in asking for the **tough assignment** and asked if he realized my expectation would be for him to **hit a home run.** He said he did and was confident he could. I told him I would think about it and let him know in two days.

I was impressed! This was a page out of my play-book and I knew when he left my office I was going to give him the job. However, I saw an opportunity to build in some added support for what he had to do.

I thought three supervisors in processing were very capable, although they had not delivered. The next day I took them to lunch, told them I was going to give them a rare opportunity, shared with them my conversation with the unit manager and asked what they would advise. After they recovered from shock, they laughed and said they thought I was going to fire them, instead I was allowing them to participate in the selection of their new boss. I said, "This is a unique opportunity. You have worked closely with him for the last three years and I'm sure, have formed an opinion of his capabilities. Because of the critical nature of this position, I need to make the best decision I can and input from you would be invaluable". I could tell they were flattered and took their new responsibility seriously. There was unanimous support for him. I was pleased. I'm not sure what I would have done if they said no. I was also pleased with the dynamic this had created. I now had three supervisors who had a vested interest in his success. I knew, they would not let him fail!

The next day, after consultation with the general manager, I offered him the processing job, reiterated my expectations and pledged whatever support he needed.

The green pens worked like magic. Overnight the underwriting environment went from looking for ways to decline an account to looking for ways to write it. The increased activity created more interaction with the home office referral unit and I found myself embroiled in a major dispute with home office underwriting.

I contended the decision to write or decline a large

account rests with the branch office and the home office's role was to provide the technical expertise to develop the program. Since there were no written rules and no one was anxious to create any, it often came down to individual account discussions. I always prevailed but in the process developed a reputation of not respecting the underwriting process. I countered that was not true. I had nothing but the utmost respect for underwriting but it had its limitations. Underwriting is not a science. It can identify the twenty percent of the best accounts in a class and the worst twenty percent, but the sixty percent in the middle is a crap shoot. Insurance is the law of large numbers which demands an ever increasing pool of money to pay losses. Stagnation in revenue growth could result in the pool being overrun with the losses of the few, so growth becomes a critical part of profitability. I was ultimately accountable for the results and would not allow the home office to supplant my authority in making the underwriting decision. I was widely criticized for my position, but it wasn't the first time I was on the unpopular side of an issue and I was sure it wouldn't be the last.

Things were falling into place. We had a long way to go, but we were headed in the right direction. Revenue started to increase, service and quality from processing was getting better and profitability was improving. I was really impressed with the new manager I had hired in processing. Things had improved a lot and morale in the department was better than I had seen.

Over the years we had become the major insurance carrier for the garbage haulers for the city. They were all independent contractors, believed to be controlled by organized crime, and handled by one agent. Losing a lot of money on the business and over the agent's objections, we decided to terminate our relationship, and began sending out non-renewal notices on our policies. The general manager started receiving death threats in the mail. Then one day a wreath was delivered to the office with a note that said, " Rest in peace." We contacted the police and the FBI and the home office hired a full time body-guard for the general manager. His office, my office and the CID department were on the first floor of our building. One day someone threw a cinder block through a window. The next day the home office had bullet proof glass installed in the GM's and my office. While watching the worker putting in the glass, I said, "I can't believe you're putting bullet proof glass in my office; if my mother knew this, she'd make me come home." He almost fell off the ladder laughing.

The Aetna's annual shareholders' meeting was scheduled during this time and a letter was received in Hartford warning the meeting would be disrupted. The meeting went on as scheduled and was attended by more plain clothes FBI agents than shareholders. The FBI interviewed several suspects and eventually the threats stopped.

I was well into my second year in the city and things were going splendidly. We were writing a ton of new business and the processing unit was performing beyond expectations. The manager had done a fantastic job and the three supervisors had stepped up in a big way to make sure he succeeded. My boss had completely changed his view of me and was now my biggest supporter. Just a few months away from retirement and nervous about an upcoming home office audit, because it would be his last, he wanted it to be a good one. I assured him we were in great shape and this would be the best audit ever for the office. He was cautiously optimistic.

Sexual harassment was a big issue at the time and home office human resources personnel were touring the country giving workshops on the rules of engagement when dealing with employees. One of my most memorable moments in New York was sitting with the boss in his office for the team wrap-up meeting. The team leader was going through a list of things that should be avoided when the general manager jumped up out of his chair, pounded the desk, and said "I'm sick of being told what I can and can't do and I remember a time when the main reason you came to work was the person you'd be necking with behind the file cabinets". The team leader was speechless. Then our boss assured her we were fine and dismissed the meeting. Since he was so close to retirement, I'm sure the home office decided to give him a pass.

My ongoing battle with home office continued, but my

position was buoyed by the success we were having and their approach had morphed into a "give him enough rope and he'll hang himself" stance, which was fine with me since I knew that wasn't likely to happen. We had started writing more and larger accounts and forming relationships with the national brokers. One of the underwriters had done a great job in this area. She approached me with the idea of forming a separate unit to deal with the national brokers only and focus on writing larger accounts. I thought it was a good idea and told her to develop a plan and I would take it forward.

    In the meantime, we had a major problem with one of the large accounts she handled. A construction company, owned by two brothers from Italy, had generated well over a quarter of a million dollars in revenue in a short period of time and our audit showed an additional premium due of over $100,000. They refused to pay it until their client paid them. We informed them that that was not the way it worked; the audit premium was due immediately or their coverage would be cancelled. Normally the agent collected premiums but the agent in this case had refused to press his client for collection, and left it up to us. We had always suspected the account was a part of the organized crime network and the agent was not willing to put himself in harms way. One of the brothers requested a meeting with me to resolve the issue. On the day of the meeting, he came into my office looking like he just left the set of the Godfather movie, and sat in a chair close to my desk. The unit manager and the underwriter joined us. We told him how the system worked, but he refused to accept our explanation, repeatedly saying it made no sense for him to pay us before he got paid. The meeting got very contentious with a lot of yelling. At one point he leaned on my desk and said "Do you know I can pick up that phone, make a call and get anything I want done in this city?" I leaned forward in my chair and said; "Then, you had better call someone to write your insurance, because we're cancelling it." With this the underwriter and the unit manager gasped. I was a bit confused by their actions. A few more choice words were exchanged and the contractor left my office. The unit manager rushed toward my desk and said, almost out of breath,

"Did you know he had a gun?" The contractor had a gun strapped to his ankle which I couldn't see, but they could. We kept watch for the next hour or so to make sure he didn't return. We cancelled the policy and never heard from them again; neither did we collect our money.

The long-awaited home office audit was scheduled and everyone was on edge, with the general manager almost unable to control himself. Having learned the value of promoting positive relationships, I contacted the team leader and arranged a dinner the night of their arrival at a very nice restaurant we frequented. I explained to the restaurant manager, whom I knew, the importance of the dinner and requested a little extra attention to the team. All my managers attended the dinner with the eight members of the audit team. We planned to take this opportunity to acquaint the team with the overall approach of the office and give them our assessment of how things stood. Given the vagary of an audit team, I wanted to give them a scenario they would be hard pressed to disprove and after a great dinner, would be more inclined to confirm. We brought out the charm and the dinner was a huge success. When leaving dinner, the team leader said in all his years doing this, no office had ever entertained the team prior to an audit, thanked us for our hospitality and said what a great time they had. Mission accomplished.

The audit went off without a hitch. We exceeded standards in every area including the dreaded error ratio. The processing manager and his team had brought it down from the mid-thirties to eight percent. The team leader commented he had rarely seen the kind of enthusiasm and collaboration that he had witnessed during this visit, which pleased me greatly. The boss was ecstatic. Four days later, when he got the official written report, he came into my office, pulled me out of my chair, gave me a grandfatherly hug, and with tears streaming down his face said, "You gave me the greatest retirement gift possible and words can't express how grateful I am". He would finish his career on top of the world, with a glowing report on the office where he had started forty years ago as a mail-boy. I'm sure he framed that report. It reminded me of the many rewards of a successful operation. **The** bottom line is one thing, but the satisfaction of a "job well done" is priceless.

I treated my staff to a celebration following the audit at the same restaurant where we entertained the audit team. The manager pulled out all the stops and a good time was had by all. Though the whole office excelled, the processing manager was the hero of the evening and his colleagues toasted him well into the night. **He had asked for the tough assignment and hit a home run**. I was proud of him and knew he had a bright future ahead. He had followed the **Five P's,** exhibited all of the characteristics of a strong leader and created an organization with all of the traits of a high-performing unit. I had spent a lot of time coaching him and he was a willing student. He would go far in his career if he continued on the same path, which I had no doubt he would.

The following day, the GM threw a party for the whole office, catered by one of the finest delis in the area. He was like a kid at Disneyland, kissing all the girls and enjoying his moment in the sun. It was fun to see.

We had a big retirement party for him, attended by a host of home office dignitaries. He was a popular general manager and a lot of people admired his accomplishments. It was extremely rare, to rise from the mailroom to the general manager's office in a company like Aetna that placed a premium on Ivy League educations and MBA's.

A lifer, the general manager of the Garden City, New York office, took over. He wanted to finish his career in the city. He was right out of the Aetna GM playbook-- super conservative, well-dressed, well-educated and not accustomed to challenging Hartford. He had heard about the success we were having and upon his arrival announced he had no plans to change anything, which was music to my ears. I did inform him of our relationship with home office underwriting and warned that he might have to show his support at some point. He said he would be happy to do that. I thought he wanted to flex his muscles his last two years on the job and I would be happy to give him the opportunity.

The underwriter's plan for the National Broker Unit advanced. She would supervise the unit and start with one other person with the understanding that additional staff would be added as they grew. They would deal with the four national brokers and focus on accounts $100,000 and up. They would still use the home office referral unit with underwriting authority remaining in the office. She projected they could write ten million dollars in premiums the first year.

I approached the new general manager with the proposal. He didn't think the home office would approve, but was willing to give his support if I wanted to try. This was the response I anticipated. I told him I didn't think we needed home office approval; that agency appointments were our responsibility and half of the brokers were already in place. Only the dedicated unit was unique. Since we were using existing job classes, there was nothing for the home office to do. He was not comfortable with this approach, and said while what I said was true, because of Aetna's reluctance to deal with brokers in any meaningful way, this would definitely raise eyebrows. I told him I agreed, but in my experience it was always better to beg for forgiveness than ask for permission and if I were he, I would implement the unit and report on it in his next quarterly report as a new initiative to improve premium growth, that we enthusiastically endorsed, and praise the underwriter for the idea. I knew I would never get him comfortable with this approach, but after telling him I would assume responsibility for any fall-out, he agreed to do it. My mantra was alive and well: **"You can get people to do almost anything if your motives are pure, you rationale convincing and sincere and the interaction takes place in an atmosphere of trust and mutual respect"**.

The underwriter selected a property specialist to work with her and the unit was off and running. The brokers were happy to see our new approach and I was sure the unit would write a lot of business.

We finished my second year in the city in fine shape. We had double digit growth and a combined ratio of ninety seven percent. The combined ratio is the main financial measure for insurance companies. It is the combination of claims paid and the cost of running the operation, including a share of home office expenses. Anything under a hundred percent in a high interest rate environment is considered good. We had a successful audit and the national broker unit was off to a great start. We were out of the garbage business, everyone was still safe and the office was positioned for several years of growth and profit.

We were running out of space and decided to move the office. After considering several options, we moved to World Trade Center Two. My office was on the 34th floor with a view of the Hudson River and the Statue of Liberty. I thought it doesn't get any better than this and how lucky I was to be at a place like this from my humble beginnings on the farm. There is a quote that says; **"you know you're happy when reality is better than your dreams". I was just about there.**

The next few months were pretty uneventful. The new general manager was settling in. Everyone was enjoying the new office. I was proud of our accomplishments which had gotten high praise. Then one day the general manager came into my office and told me the head of field management would be visiting in a couple of days and wanted to spend some time with me. The general managers reported to field management so this was not unusual. I knew the head of the department, but didn't have a particularly close relationship with him so I was looking forward to getting to know him better.

When he arrived he spent some time with the general manager then came into my office. He was very complimentary of what we had done and said he personally liked my aggressive style and wished the company had more leaders willing to challenge the status quo. Then he said he was there to offer me the general manager's job in Syracuse, New York. It was the smallest of the sixty offices, located in a very conservative area where insurance was historically a profitable business, but had experienced difficulty growing. He thought my aggressive style would help achieve the kind of growth the company needed. I accepted. He congratulated me and pledged whatever support I needed. I thanked him and assured him I would call if I needed help.

As soon as he left, the general manager came into my office, congratulated me, and said "At thirty-seven you have to be one of the youngest general managers the company ever had." I told him I was honored and looked forward to the opportunity.

I was leaving the city after a stay of less than three years. Albeit relatively short, it was packed with incredible experiences. My **Five P's** strategy was right on, the **Leadership Characteristics** were absolutely the correct ones and the **High Performing Organizations' Traits** had proven to deliver superior results. I couldn't wait to get to Syracuse where I would run the whole show and put them into action all over again.

I had a great going away party attended by employees and several agents. I got numerous gifts, including a set of golf clubs. Even though I didn't play golf, the employees said since Syracuse was such a small town, I would have to curtail my partying and find a new activity; they thought golf should be it. As excited as I was about Syracuse, leaving the people was always hard and there were lots of tears all around. I took some degree of comfort in knowing I was leaving the office in much better shape than when I arrived and a lot of what we put in place would continue.

THE BOSS ARRIVES

My confidence was at an all-time high as I headed to Syracuse. New York proved, beyond the shadow of a doubt that my philosophies of performance, leadership, and organizational effectiveness was right on target and produced superior results. I regretted Ollie wasn't around to see the success of his experiment and hoped one day I would get the chance to share the experience. Patience was never a virtue for me and I couldn't wait to get started.

I bought a two-bedroom townhouse, with a garage, which I would discover later, was a must in Syracuse because of the winter weather. It was also an easy fifteen to twenty minute commute to my office, located downtown on Salina Street, the main thoroughfare in the city.

I received a warm welcome in the office. My reputation had preceded me. The employees were as frustrated as anyone about their inability to grow and were looking forward to a different brand of leadership. They also understood the magnitude of that challenge in their current environment. Syracuse was in a severe economic slump with no end in sight, leaving insurance companies battling over an ever-decreasing number of businesses and the shrinking of those that survived. In most territories our market share was one to two percent. To succeed in Syracuse it would have to be ten percent or better, a tall order in a price-sensitive business like insurance. I was reminded of one of the slogans for the armed services: **"The Difficult We Do Immediately, The Impossible Takes A Little Longer"**.

Part of the training for all new general managers was to spend a week with one of the veterans in the office of your choice. I picked Richmond, not for the training opportunity, but for the chance to take a victory lap of sorts. Few general managers came from Richmond and I couldn't resist returning to where it all started. Many people in the company watched this selection closely and my choice baffled everyone since the Richmond general manager was the dean of the traditionalists. They didn't know this was more about celebration and had nothing to do with training. My brand of leadership was so different from the norm none of the existing GM's could be helpful.

I decided not to get a briefing on the backgrounds and performance of my new staff. I received some bad information in the city, so I had little confidence in the system. All I got was name, length of employment and the department they managed. I shared this with them when I arrived and told them I wouldn't look at a personnel file for at least six months so they didn't have to be concerned about any impression I may have formed from their past performance. I shared with them my teamwork philosophy and told them while their primary responsibility was for their department they would all be held accountable for the overall performance of the office. I impressed upon them the importance of tapping into the talents of all one hundred and twenty-five people to develop the plan we would need to accomplish our goals.

My vision for the Syracuse Office was: **"Create a High Performing Organization That Maximizes the Talents of all Employees to Deliver Excellent Customer Service, a Sustained Growth Rate And Superior Returns on Invested Assets"**. I shared this with them and told them they should discuss it, debate it and if they didn't agree with it or had suggestions that would make it better, let me know. Then I charged them with developing the strategic plan to support that vision, getting input from the entire organization. I had only two criteria: 1. We would never develop a plan that showed an underwriting loss 2. We would never develop a plan that didn't show growth. Everything else was on the table.

I then met with all the employees and got a warm reception. I shared with them a version of my vision since it hadn't been finalized, laid out what we had to accomplish, and told them I was counting on them to be full participants in what we had to do. I also told them I had complete confidence in their ability to succeed and pledged an exciting fun-filled adventure ahead. At my insistence we agreed I would be called Al and not Mr. Austin. They applauded.

My secretary was very uncomfortable calling me Al, so I made a deal with her. I had an option to get a new secretary and told her she could keep her job only if she called me Al. She agreed on one condition: that she could say Mr. Austin's office when she answered the phone. I agreed.

My staff got busy working on our new strategy and I headed to Richmond. The first person I saw when I entered the office was the human resource person who had conducted my first interview for a trainee job. She welcomed me back to Richmond, congratulated me on the promotion to general manager and asked if that meant she had to call me Mr. Austin now. I said, "No, it means you are very good at selecting new employees." She blushed.

The GM was known throughout the company for his expansive vocabulary. He kept one of those oversized dictionaries on a stand in his office and said he studied a page every day he was in the office. He also had a very loud baritone voice and I could tell liked to intimidate people. We exchanged pleasantries and made plans to meet the following day. I headed to the claim department and was surprised to see everyone was still there. Aetna was known as "Mother Aetna" because it took care of its employees for their entire work life. I took all the supervisors to dinner that night and we had fun catching up. They couldn't remember the last time a new GM came from the Richmond office.

The second day, as I sat in the GM's office, his secretary came in and said my secretary had called asking for Al. The GM immediately reprimanded me for allowing her to call me Al. He was appalled when I told him I insisted on it. He said, "You'll have to change that as soon as you return. You can't have employees calling you Al". I further upset him when I asked "Will that make me a better general manager?"

When I returned to Syracuse it was obvious my staff was struggling with coming up with a workable strategy. I was not surprised since I knew it was going to require some **bold** moves into **unfamiliar** territory and I would have to get them comfortable with this approach. I had to dispel some of the long-held Aetna beliefs about how we conduct business and put forth an alternative they could believe in. Companies like Aetna had promoted a value-added approach to writing business that said potential clients would pay more to be insured by a reputable company that provided great service. For that reason, and a sense of loyalty for the support we provided, agents would place their business with us. My New York experience taught me otherwise. Ninety percent of our products were commodity products and the only differentiator is price. Even at the higher end of the market, the best quality accounts were not going to pay more just to be insured with us. To be successful we would have to compete on price. That being said, if you were going to compete on price, you had to be sure the quality of the business you wrote was top notch, the top twenty percent.

I had always believed you were much more likely to make money on a quality book of business underpriced than an average book of business at any price. This position contributed to the issues I had with home office. To make this approach work we had to have an aggressive claim operation committed to paying the right amount for only those claims we owed; no compromises. There was always a question about how far to go when disputing claims before endangering customer relationships. My answer to that question was a bifurcation of claim handling. First, first-party claimants, the people who pay premiums to protect their homes, cars, and buildings associated with their businesses were our customers. We should treat them well and most of the time resolve disputed issues in their favor. Third party claimants, those we became liable to because of the actions of our insured's were not our customers and in most cases were trying to take advantage of the system. We should treat them equitably and fairly, but never pay a dime more than we owe and be willing to defend our position with all of the tools at our disposal. This was not the prevailing view at Aetna.

To execute this strategy we needed to align ourselves with the best agents in the business and provide them with the highest level of service they could imagine. We were going to be asking for their best clients and they would expect a lot in return. Whether agents were customers or not was an unresolved question in the P & C business for years. My answer was agents are not **our customers,** they are **our partners,** which makes them more important than customers because our fates were interdependent. The people who pay the bills are our customers and we share a responsibility to them with our agents.

We discussed and debated this for days, sometimes well into the night. The biggest concern was the reaction of home office. This was so far away from the prevailing view we were certain to attract the fury of Hartford. I told them they were absolutely right and it was my job to provide cover and fend off any attack from Hartford. I also told them even Hartford would be hard pressed to attack an operation that was growing and making money and that is exactly what we were going to do. The underwriting manager was skeptical. While he bought the theory, he questioned our ability to execute it. I told him that was a matter of knowledge and will and if he didn't feel up to the task I would understand. The marketing manager and the administration manager were onboard, but the former's timid endorsement concerned me. The bond manager was anxious to get started. The claims manager was going to retire in thirty days, so I asked his superintendent to be at all meetings since she was a strong candidate for his replacement. She was the most enthusiastic and said the claim department could deliver. The underwriting manager was capable, but I would have to stay close to him until he got fully committed, or replace him. I decided to give him a chance.

We wrote nineteen million dollars in business, and had 149 agents, so one of our objectives was to trim our agent pool and focus on people who could give us large volumes of business. Also, the two largest agents in Syracuse didn't do business with us and that would have to change. We set some minimum premium requirements and started to reduce the list. This is always a painful process because some of these were small operations that had done business with us for years. We did everything we could to promote mergers and acquisitions that would allow them to stay in business. Then we went to work on the two large agents to get them onboard. Haylor, Fryer and Coon, the largest, brought a small personal lines Aetna agent. We used this to convince them to sign a commercial contract. The second largest agent was the Young Agency. After several meetings and sharing our plans, we got them to sign up.

I called an all-employee meeting to review the strategy and get everyone on board. I knew it would take more than one meeting so this was mainly to get the conversation started. I would use my "management by wandering about" approach to have many one-on-one conversations with the underwriters. Underwriters always want to write business, so we had to get them comfortable with pricing it aggressively when needed. I would also have to spend time with claims to reassure them I understood a tougher stance would generate more lawsuits, but I assured them that was okay and temporary, because as soon as plaintiff attorneys realized we were serious, they would stop taking Aetna cases and move on to easier pickings. I wasn't concerned about claims because the superintendent was fully committed to our new approach, and she was very likely to become the next manager.

Next we arranged a meeting with all of the agents. Unlike the City where our agents were concentrated in a relatively small geographic area, ours were spread out from the Canadian border to the Pennsylvania border, and would take a year to visit. We billed it as an introductory meeting for me and told them I would lay out our plans for the territory, strategy for achieving it and the role they would play. All the underwriters, marketing reps and claim reps attended. I wanted them to hear what the agents were hearing.

The agency meeting was going to be critical for our strategy so I took a little extra care in preparing my speech. At the appointed time, dressed in one of my best tailor-made suits, without a single note, I talked for an hour with the full attention of the audience the entire time. The underwriting manager gave a brief introduction and I shared more of my background, including that I grew up on a farm in Virginia. I think this served to offset some of their concern about me coming from the Big Apple. The difference between the city and upstate New York is like night and day and there is always a bit of disdain among people from upstate for City people.

 I told them I was sent to Syracuse to bring a more aggressive style to a very profitable territory where our growth was stagnant in a shrinking market and we had to figure out how to change that or close the office. Closing the office, I said was not an option for me because I was too young to retire, so we had to grow in a big way. That was going to require a significant change in how we conducted business. Then I told them we were going to increase our market share from roughly one and a half percent to ten percent and we were going to do it by writing the best business in the territory, which meant the best business in their offices. To accomplish this we would provide the most competitive price on the street and our underwriters would go to the limits for good business. In exchange for this I asked they give us only their best, which met with some scorn. I told them we were going to provide the best service imaginable and create an ease of doing business that would reduce their operating cost to a level where they couldn't afford to not do business with us. I told them we did not consider them customers, but partners and as such they were more important to us than a customer and we would forge strong partnerships with the best in their ranks. Then I told them we were reducing the number of agents we did business with and profiled our desirable partner. My closing highlighted a high-performing organization with smart aggressive enthusiastic people producing superior results for them and Aetna and a joy to work with! Then I said, "I want you to do business with us not because you like us, but because you're afraid not to: We're going to be that good. Loyalty has proved to be an ineffective strategy, so we are replacing it with relationships built on sound business practices that foster your success and ours. If it turns out you like us in the process, and I hope you do, that's a bonus". There was polite applause. I wanted to shock them and let them know things were going to change in a big way and they needed to be on the right side of that change or their relationship with us, and their business was in jeopardy. Mission accomplished. The lively question and answer period left no doubt they got the message. The next day my phone was ringing off the hook from agents requesting meetings. The strategy had been launched and we were off and running.

To say this was a bold strategy would be a gross understatement. This was the kind of move that would be wildly successful or end my career. I wasn't concerned about growing, but the risk to profitability was daunting. The base or manual rates actuaries supplied to underwriting represented what the average account in that class should pay. Companies also used flexible rating plans that allowed the underwriter to credit or debit a base rate based on the quality of the account relative to the average; a judgement call, supported by how the account ran its operation. In our case, underwriters could debit or credit an account as much as seventy-five percent. With our strategy we had to be absolutely sure we didn't leave any money on the table. This would require ongoing knowledge of what our competitors were doing and total commitment from the agent who would be at the point of sale. With our narrow margins there was no room for error; execution at every level needed to be flawless.

After the agency meeting the marketing manager resigned. He didn't feel comfortable with our strategy or our ability to execute it. The claim manager retired and I promoted the superintendent to that position. I felt good about this since she was an enthusiastic supporter of the strategy from day one and having observed her over the past few months, I had no doubt she could deliver. She knew the claim business inside and out, was respected by the legal community and was aggressive in her approach to claim handling. She had two supervisors who were very capable and they shared a close relationship.

Replacing the marketing manager was not so easy. I interviewed several candidates, but found no one suitable. I knew it was going to be difficult because our strategy was so different from anything they were familiar with. I got several calls from agents recommending promoting the supervisor in the department. He was a local product and had asked to be considered for the job. I had gotten to know him pretty well and thought given the situation, he would be the best choice. Promoting from within is always a popular choice. When I announced his promotion I stressed the influence the agents' recommendations had on his selection and said I expected them to participate heavily in his success.

The underwriting manager got comfortable with the strategy and was completely committed. I was relieved since he was highly regarded by our agents and employees and would be a key player in our approach. The team was set and I spent hours/days coaching them on the **characteristics of great leaders** and the **traits of high performing organizations**. In addition they got to observe me on a daily basis hanging out with underwriters, marketing reps and claims reps seeing the easy exchange of information with no reservation to disagree with me when appropriate. To get people comfortable about arguing with the boss, I used to create debates in public view.

We were moving fast and getting results almost immediately. Agents tested us to see if we were serious and found we were. I had assigned our two best marketing reps to the two big agents we appointed and they were delivering in spades. I was getting the expected flack from Hartford but was able to fend them off. I felt certain if we could get twelve months into the strategy the results would be enough to give us some space.

Everybody was in overdrive. I was visiting agents, getting them on board, collecting feedback and terminating relationships with those that didn't make the cut. These were always team visits with the underwriting manager, the marketing manager and quite often the claim manager accompanying me.

All field offices had a big outing each year for its top agents. This was a two-day event that had some business, but mostly pleasure and always held at a nice venue. Ours was held at the Otesaga Resort on Otsego Lake in Cooperstown, New York, a great resort with a world class golf course, tennis courts and fabulous food. My first year, we had twenty-two agencies and forty people attended. We also invited three people from home office, one from underwriting, marketing and field management. The agenda usually included an early lunch the first day followed by golf or some other activity and a big dinner that night, with golf and lunch the next day. The highlight of the dinner was the general manager's state of the office speech. I told them we were well into our new strategy and results were impressive. Our growth rate was forty-five percent and losses had not spiked. We had terminated thirty agencies with more to come and service levels were at an all-time high. I thanked them for their support and announced we expected profit-sharing payments to be at record levels for the year.

We used a profit-sharing arrangement with our agents to give them the opportunity to share in the profit of their book of business. The amounts varied based on the size of the book and the amount of the losses. This got big applause. The mood overall was very upbeat. Agents liked our new strategy because it protected their existing clients and gave them a powerful tool to compete for new business. Once the shock wore off, they realized that while our new strategy was radical, properly executed, it was good for all parties. In a short time they had gone from "how dare they" to "those Aetna people really got their act together."

After dinner several agents approached me and said they heard I was a poker player, to which I replied that I was known to place a bet or two. They suggested we start a game and I was more than happy to oblige. It ended up being a pretty high stakes game that lasted well into the morning. I hadn't played poker in some time but did very well. We parted friends, had a quick nap, ate breakfast and headed to the golf course.

Word of the poker game reached Hartford before I got back to my office. I got a call from the head of marketing, asking if I thought holding a high-stakes poker game at a company function was appropriate. I informed him the poker game was not my idea, was not planned, and I participated to accommodate the request of our agents. I said I thought it was appropriate under those circumstances. The games would become a permanent part of the annual outing for the duration of my stay in Syracuse.

We finished my first year in Syracuse with forty-five percent growth and a combined ratio of ninety-seven percent. My staff was practicing the characteristics of great leaders and we had a high-performing organization with all of the necessary traits. I felt really good about where we were. I had a high degree of confidence in our strategy to begin with and this was the confirmation I wanted.

To represent Aetna as a good corporate citizen and promote our brand outside the boundaries of insurance, I encouraged all employees to be involved with their community. We looked for things with the greatest impact. One day an employee came into my office and said she saw a story on the local news the rape crisis center in the county where she lived was losing its state funding and needed fifteen thousand dollars to keep its doors open. She thought we should give them the money. I told her to check out the story, get all of the details and we would consider it. She did and found state budget cuts resulted in the county losing its funding. Since it was a small county, there was no other source. I agreed to give them the money, and the next day after the news of the funding cut aired, the TV station interviewed me and reported our gift. We got tons of positive press.

As general manager, I played my role in community involvement. Aetna had a major presence in a city fighting to preserve its downtown. I got to know the mayor and was on every commission he had. I was also a regular speaker at business and civic functions on a wide range of issues. I was even invited to speak at Cornell University's International conference for the hospitality industry. Governor Mario Cuomo appointed me to the Advisory Board for the Department of Business Permits and Regulatory Assistance. The Chief Justice of the Northern District Federal Court named me, the only non-lawyer he appointed, to serve on its Advisory Group.

Our monthly all-employee meetings were always lively and mostly celebratory. Results were so good we spent a lot of time patting each other on the back. However, I always had an educational message. Before one meeting, I read Noel Tichy's book, The Transformational Leader. One of the things he discusses is the critical need for successful companies to stay aware of changes in its environment no matter how subtle. He used the boiled frog theory to illustrate what happens to companies who fail to track changes. The theory says that if you put a frog in a pan of cool water, set the pan on a Bunsen burner and turn the flame up very slowly the frog will remain in the pan and boil to death because the changes in its environment are so subtle it does not detect them soon enough. But if you drop a frog in a pan of boiling water, it will react, jump out and save itself, because the change is so drastic. I cautioned everyone against becoming a boiled frog. Everyone thought this was a great analogy and there was a lot of discussion. Then one of the underwriters said, "Al we should do something with that." I asked what she had in mind. She said she didn't know, but there had to be something. I said get a few of your friends, together and come up with something and we'll do it.

Two weeks later the group came into my office with their plan. They had designed a cartoon that showed two frogs in a pan of water with flames under it. One frog was sitting with his arms draped over the side of the pan relaxing holding a drink with a red umbrella. The second frog was leaping out of the pan and carrying a briefcase with AETNA on the side. It was brilliant. Their plan was to create tee shirts with the cartoon on the front and Aetna Commercial Insurance on the back. An attached card would explain the theory. They had found a manufacturer and wanted to order five hundred to distribute to agents and employees. I loved it. We would reorder twice. Everybody wanted a boiled frog tee shirt and we became known as the boiled frog company. I can't put a number on how much this improved revenue, but I know it had an impact. Tapping into all the talents of all employees is powerful stuff!

In the late eighties during a February blizzard in one of the largest fires in Syracuse history, the Lafayette Country Club, which we insured, burned to the ground. The claim manager was on the scene before the fire was out and I, along with the agent, was there shortly after. Large property losses are sometimes difficult to settle because public adjusters try to solicit property owners to hire them to provide representation in working with the insurance company for ten percent of the final settlement. Since property losses are pretty finite in value, the adjuster's ten percent has to come from inflating the claim or the property owner gives up ten percent of the settlement. This was going to be a three-to-five million dollar loss, and I knew adjusters would be beating down the property owners' door. The claim manager and I cornered the agent, still at the site of the fire, and told him we had to keep adjusters out of this loss because if they siphoned ten percent off the top of this claim, settlement was going to be difficult. I asked the agent to arrange a meeting with the board of directors that night so we could discuss with them what would happen and convince them they didn't need an adjuster.

The claim manager, the underwriting manager and I attended the meeting. We brought a check for five hundred thousand dollars with us as a sign of good faith, explained the coverage they had, reviewed the settlement process and assured the board we would proceed with their best interest at the forefront. I also advised them they had the option to hire an adjuster at any point during the process if they felt they were being treated unfairly. They agreed not to hire an adjuster.

At our next all-employee meeting I updated everyone on the loss and said we would be hard pressed to make our profit goals for the year with such a large loss. Then one of the underwriters spoke up and said, "Al, the good news is it happened in February which gives us ten months to make up the loss payment." As the leader, this was exactly the response you would hope for. This signified a sense of ownership and "can do" attitude every leader hopes to have. We finished the year with a forty-five percent increase in revenue and a combined ratio of ninety-three percent. We settled the claim for well over three million dollars without the involvement of a public adjuster and received rave reviews from the local media for how it was handled. We never had to worry about public adjusters being involved in our claims again.

We were growing at a record pace, adding staff and running out of office space. Our lease was coming up so we started the search for a new office. The trend at the time was to move to the suburbs where parking was free and the environment more relaxed than the city. We decided to follow the trend. The city had built a large multi-use facility in downtown and was desperately looking for an anchor tenant with little success, since it was almost impossible for them to compete with the rents being charged by the suburban locations. The mayor called me and said, "You have to help me out." I said, "Put together your best deal and I'll consider it." He came back with a deal that included free parking but would cost us a million dollars more a year in rents. Our leases were negotiated by the home office, so I would have to convince Hartford to pay a million dollars more a year to stay downtown. I called an all-employee meeting to discuss the situation and get a feel for how everyone felt. There was overwhelming support for staying downtown. I cautioned this would be a hard sell, but I would try. After all I still knew **you can get people to do almost anything if your motives are pure, your rationale convincing and sincere and the discussion takes place in an atmosphere of trust and mutual respect.**

I flew to Hartford with the mayor to make our case. We met with the head of the property lease department and representatives from field management, including my boss. The mayor made a passionate plea about what this would mean to the continued revitalization of downtown Syracuse and without us would be a significant setback. I reviewed the positive impact this would have on our image and noted the publicity would generate additional revenue, hard to quantify but nonetheless real. I also assured them I was confident our bottom-line could take the hit and not adversely affect our profitability. After a vigorous discussion we agreed to stay downtown.

This was big news and when the announcement was made, I became an instant hero. I got calls and letters from local politicians and businessmen thanking Aetna for its commitment to downtown and helping the city out of a very difficult situation. I was interviewed on local television several times and there was a huge banner, stretched across Salina Street, the main thoroughfare, welcoming Aetna to The Galleries of Syracuse. The publicity we got was priceless and I knew would have a positive impact on the bottom-line.

Our growth and profit were astounding. We went from being the smallest office to being in the top ten for size and number one for profit. Morale in the office was so good, going into the office every day was more like a party than work. Home office was baffled by what was happening, but not about to try to change it, at least so we thought.

Then one day the underwriting manager got a call from an assistant vice-president from home office underwriting saying they had received a complaint, with a copy to the state insurance department, from an agent in our territory that our pricing was unreasonable, that he had competed against us on four accounts and lost all four. The AVP said his boss wanted us to forward the four files to home office so they could respond to the complaint.

Company protocol was branch offices responded to complaints. The underwriting manager came into my office, told me about the phone call and asked what he should do. I told him to call the AVP back, tell him we were unaware of the complaint, that per company protocol we would be happy to respond, but we were not going to send four files to Hartford for their response. Recognizing the firestorm this was going to create, the underwriting manager asked if I was sure this is what we wanted to do. I said, "Absolutely, we can't have the home office second guessing the decisions our underwriters have made that are consistent with our strategy, unless we're willing to abandon that strategy which we're not." I did tell him to invite the AVP to Syracuse where he could review our overall approach and judge those four files in that context.

When the underwriting manager left to make the call, I called an attorney friend to get the definition of insubordination, since that was one of the grounds for immediate termination. I knew this was going to be a defining moment and I couldn't afford to create an indefensible position. The attorney assured me insubordination was refusal to follow an order of your superior. Since the head of underwriting was not in the-chain-of-command, my refusal wouldn't qualify.

I had been battling the senior vice-president of underwriting since my days in the City. He had no respect for my approach to the business and was always looking for things to bolster his position. Minutes after the underwriting manager made his call, my phone rang. It was the Senior Vice-President of Underwriting. There was no greeting. He said "What the (expletive deleted) do you mean you're not sending the four files to Hartford?" I replied, "Company protocol is for branch offices to respond to complaints, that if he would forward the letter, we would be happy to do that, but if he preferred to come to Syracuse and discuss those four files in the context of our overall strategy, he was welcome to visit our office." He asked if I had discussed this with my boss and I said no. He suggested I do so and hung up.

I called my boss and told him what happened. He asked if I had lost my mind. I assured him I hadn't, and if I was to remain the general manager, I couldn't send the files even if I wanted to. We had an unusual, aggressive strategy and I had pledged to my employees I would protect them against second-guessing by Hartford. If I sent the files, their **trust** in me would be destroyed and I could no longer function. He understood, warned me of the dangers ahead, said I was entering uncharted waters, but he would support me to the extent he could. I called the senior vice-president of underwriting, told him I had discussed this with my boss and my decision had not changed. He hung up without a word.

The next day I received a call from one of the underwriting directors, informing me he was assembling a pricing audit team and they would be in Syracuse next week. Unlike normal audit procedures, we would not get an advanced list of file. Instead they would identify the files in Hartford, and I should have someone available to pull them once the team arrived. I knew him pretty well. He had a great reputation as an underwriter and was a fixture in the underwriter training programs. While I wouldn't say he supported our strategy, he was probably the only one in Hartford that gave it any merit at all. He had also started his Aetna career in the same office I had, Richmond, Virginia.

The battle had been joined. The tension in the office was unlike anything I had ever seen. Despite my best efforts to reassure everybody, they knew what was at stake and even if I was the only one fired, life would never be the same. I even pulled out one of my old Lee Woodruff quotes: **"Unless it's fatal, it's no big**

deal", but nothing seemed to relieve the pressure. I knew then this would just have to play out.

The ten auditors arrived and they appeared as stressed as the people in the office. This was serious business and everybody knew it. I met individually with the underwriting director to go over what they were going to do and review our strategy with him again. I told him you are going to find accounts that are high quality and priced aggressively because that's what our underwriters are expected to do. I also told him he would find well-documented files concerning the reasons for the pricing used. In addition to the file reviews, the team would also interview some of the underwriters. This was a bit unusual, but they wanted to gauge if the underwriters really understood the strategy or were just following orders. I had no objections to this because I was confident they were well-versed in the strategy and the supporting rationale.

I didn't sleep much that week and I know the underwriting manager didn't, but Friday finally arrived, and the team leader was ready for the wrap-up. They had reviewed over two hundred files and found only one that had losses. The team leader commented on how unusual that was for a standard commercial operation and that it was a testament to the account selection process our underwriters used. He then stated the file documentation was impeccable with clear rationale for all pricing decisions. He did say our pricing was extremely aggressive. On our most volatile line of business, general liability, the pricing on the accounts they reviewed was an average forty-three percent of manual or base rates. However, they were all in compliance with our filed rating plans. The underwriter interviews were impressive. They not only understood the strategy and the rationale, but also the interdependence and collaboration with claim necessary for its success. He ended by saying we had an impressive operation and should be proud of what we had accomplished. We would get his final written report in a few days.

The relief on the underwriting manager's face was visible and as soon as the team left the building, we had an all-employee meeting. I shared the results with everybody, congratulated them on a job well-done, appointed some people to plan the party for next week and gave everybody the rest of the day off. The celebration started immediately and hardly anyone left the office. The conversation was all about the experience and how we had withstood a full-force attack and come out smelling like a rose. I felt pride in what we had accomplished and seeing the people revel in their moment of glory. I had said before, "**The bottom-line is one thing, but the joy that comes from a job well done is priceless**". The final report came in a few days and the closing sentence was etched in my mind forever. After twenty pages reviewing the finding, the director said, "Yes they are giving it away, but they're making a ton of money doing it!"

A few weeks later I was attending a company function when the Senior Vice-President of underwriting came up to me and said he was glad things worked out well and he hoped I didn't think this was a witch hunt. I looked him squarely in the eyes and said I knew it was a witch hunt and I would never forgive him for what he put me and my office through, but as far as I was concerned, it was over.

Shortly after I left the City, I started dating the underwriter that started the national broker unit. Our relationship got serious pretty quickly and in November 1990 we were married. My bachelor days were over and I couldn't have been happier.

1990 was a spectacular year for the office. We grew by thirty-eight percent and had an unheard of combined ratio of eighty-four! We had moved into the top five for size and maintained a firm grip on the number one spot for profitability.

We always had one big sales meeting a year for all of our agents and I told the marketing manager we needed to do something special to celebrate our record year. Roughly two hundred people from our agents, my staff, the marketing reps and maybe one or two underwriters would be there. We decided to be both patriotic and appreciative since the Gulf War had started. During this time, multi-media presentations were popular so we hired a local firm to put together two presentations. Our opening presentation featured pictures of relatives of our agents and employees serving in the war, set to Ray Charles' rendition of

America. After the meeting, we closed with candid shots of our agents set to Bette Midler's, "Wind Beneath My Wings." We had arranged to have all branch employees enter the auditorium during the closing piece and line up along the walls. As the closing piece ended, the lights slowly came up and the employees applauded. We got rave reviews from our agents and the local media.

In the spring of 1991, my wife and I planned a May vacation in Aruba and St. Martens with two other couples. In April the executive assistant for Aetna's CEO called to say he wanted to visit our office in May. I asked if we could pick another date since I was going to be on vacation and she said that was not possible, but I didn't have to be there because the CEO wanted to spend time with some agents and employees. He would arrive Wednesday around lunch, meet with the office managers, have dinner that night with some agents, have an all-employee meeting Thursday morning and be gone by lunch. I told her she didn't know me very well if she thought for one minute I would be in St Marten's when the CEO was visiting my office. I knew him pretty well from various meetings and he was impressed by what we had accomplished in Syracuse, but we were not particularly close. I decided to make a quick trip back to the office and return to my vacation as soon as he left.

Having the CEO visit Syracuse was a big deal and the employees were determined to show him how the best office in the country operated. I picked five of our best agents to have dinner with him, at the best restaurant in town, and asked the owner to go all out. He did, including preparing a personalized Aetna menu with a special wine list. With my plans in place, I left for my abbreviated vacation in St Marten.

Tuesday, I returned to Syracuse and doubled-checked the arrangements for the CEO's visit. He arrived in the office promptly at one o'clock. I gave him a brief tour then he settled in a conference room with me and my staff. There was no agenda since he liked to keep these loose and informal so we had a lively discussion for about three hours, including presenting him with a boiled frog tee shirt. He got a kick out of that story.

Dinner was superb and the agents had nothing but praise

for Aetna. At one point the CEO even said, "Things can't be that good." But they were.

The next day's all-employee meeting was lively with lots of questions and comments about various issues. He enjoyed the give and take. When it was over, I walked him out to his limo. He said how much he appreciated me interrupting my vacation and although I didn't have to, if he were in my shoes, he would have come back too. He said that I should make sure the company paid any expenses associated with my return and asked if there was anything else he could do. I told him I left my pregnant wife in St. Marten and I thought it would be nice if when she returned he sent her a dozen roses. He said he would definitely do that and instructed his assistant to make a note. I flew to Aruba feeling good about the visit. Making a positive impression on the CEO is never a bad thing, and sending my wife flowers would give him a story he could re-tell many times.

The day after we returned from Aruba, my wife received two dozen red roses, from the CEO with a hand written note apologizing for taking me away and thanking her for her understanding. At every management meeting after that, if I was in the audience, from the podium, the CEO singled me out and told the group he had sent flowers to only two women, his wife and mine.

My first mentor, my boss In Newark, had lived up to expectations and through a progression of promotions, had ascended to the presidency of the property and casualty division. I stayed in close contact with him over the years and our relationship was tighter than ever. He had watched my rise through the ranks and supported me as he could. He called me after the visit and told me how impressed the CEO was with the Syracuse operation.

The CEO's vision for Aetna was a company that was **"Quick, Flexible and Right"**. The world was becoming a very complex place where long term strategic planning was difficult. He said successful companies had to identify emerging trends quickly and respond immediately to marketplace demands with products and services customers wanted. We were entering an era of "Permanent White Water" that would require speed and agility from successful competitors. This was the prevailing view in corporate America at the time. The excitement around emerging technologies had created a whirlwind of expectations around what the future could hold.

Mike Hammer had introduced the world to **process reengineering** which promised to squeeze all inefficiencies out of the most complex processes. Our CEO was committed. I was not. While I agreed we were entering an era of "Permanent White Water," the answer to speed and agility was not technology per se, but a Theory Y management approach that fully engaged all employees in new product development and service delivery. I once said; **"The improvements in productivity realized by the invention of the microchip pale in comparison to the potential of a fully engaged workforce."** Empowered employees would not tolerate inefficiency and with the aid of the new technologies would become more effective than ever in delivering superior results. Reengineering focused exclusively on the process with no regard for the human factor; a situation I didn't believe was sustainable. This debate would rage on for years.

To promote his vision, our CEO reorganized the company into strategic business units to serve customer segments. We had SBU's for NAD, Standard Commercial, Small Commercial, Bond, Private Passenger Auto and a Homeowner SBU. A new matrix management model with field offices similarly structured, with the field managers reporting into the home office, was installed. The general manager position became more of a high level relationship manager to coordinate distribution for all of the SBU's. The claim department was set up as a support unit completely separate from the branch offices and in most cases moved off-site to large service centers.

I didn't agree with the changes. While I thought the SBU structure could work, it would require a level of enlightened leadership at every level we didn't have. Matrix organizations are hard to manage and the dangers of creating silos, most often detrimental to the business, are great. My biggest concern, however, was the isolation of the claim department. At Aetna, this organization of seven thousand people, who paid out four-to-five billion dollars a year, would no longer be a part of the normal discussion on results, strategies or anything else affecting the business. My experience in Syracuse had taught me claim was an intimate part of a successful operation. My old friend, who had been head of NAD, was running the claim department and he supported the new approach, so I lost that argument and the new structure was implemented.

On August 8, 1991 my wife gave birth to Nicholas Louis Austin and nothing else seemed to matter. My priorities took a sudden shift and my life was forever changed. My mother had passed away in 1987 after a long battle with heart disease, but when my wife arrived home from the hospital three of my sisters were there to assist her with the first Austin boy since 1948.

The reorganization was in full swing. Fortunately, in Syracuse the impact was minor. We added a position for small commercial manager who was one of our marketing reps and a manager for personal lines. We were in the same space and they all reported to me. Home office was not going to interfere with our site, which suited me fine. We were on target to become the second largest branch office by the end of 1992 and still the most profitable. We went from the smallest office at nineteen millions dollars and would finish the year at eighty-five million. In those six years our highest combined ratio was ninety-seven percent. We had reduced the number of agents from one hundred and forty-nine to fifty and took an agency that we hadn't done business with from zero to almost thirty million dollars and made them Aetna's largest commercial agent. We had again validated the effectiveness of the **Five P's, the Leadership Characteristics and the High Performing Organization Traits.**

One day, while sitting in my office skimming Mike Hammer's book my secretary rang to tell me the president's assistant was on the phone for me. I picked up and she said he wanted to see me and would send a company plane to pick me up for a meeting in his office tomorrow morning. I said I would be there. I was half-way expecting the call. I had been in the home office a couple of weeks earlier and spent some time with the head of the small commercial SBU, another friend and contact. He asked if I would consider taking a job as the vice-president of marketing in his SBU. I told him I planned to retire from the general manager position, but that was changing so I would consider an offer from him. I thought the president was going to offer me that job.

The plane ride was nice. It was my first time on one of the corporate jets. I had taken the helicopter several times and found that enjoyable as well. A limo picked me up in Hartford and took me to the home office where a security guard escorted me to the eighth floor, where I had never been before. The president shared the floor with the CEO. He was waiting in the conference room. He said the results we achieved in Syracuse were nothing short of phenomenal, and the strategy interesting. He reviewed my battles with home office and said there were few people as outspoken and my ideas had not fallen on deaf ears. The home office was in the midst of some major changes and they needed people like me to help shape that change. Then he said the CEO and the board of directors have asked me to offer you the position of SBU head for the private passenger automobile SBU. It is a one point two billion dollar business that is declining and unprofitable with thirty five-hundred employees and we would like you to lead the turn-around. He emphasized no general manager had ever been promoted to a business head without at least one interim stop. I should consider this the board's unparalleled expression of confidence and he hoped I would accept.

I was speechless. This caught me completely by surprise. I was going from an eighty-five million dollar operation with one hundred and sixty employees to lead an area where I had no experience or training. I was familiar with the problems of this SBU and aware it got a lot of attention from the CEO who had his own ideas about how it should be run. So I told the president I would love to take the position, but only with the understanding I would fix it my way. My experience in the City and in Syracuse gave me a high degree of confidence in my approach to leadership and the major issues facing this SBU called for an approach that could tap into the hearts and minds of all thirty- five hundred employees. With that wealth of talent, I was sure we could restore growth and profit to the business. The president said he had anticipated that condition and everybody had agreed I would be given the latitude to run the business the way I felt would deliver the best results. I said yes, he congratulated me and we had a long discussion on how far we both had come.

My escort, the guard showed up, ushered me back to the limo and I was off to the airport. I later asked the president the reason for all the secrecy and he said for high-level appointments like this, it was critical to avoid rumors and my being seen leaving the executive tower, would attract attention. They thought this would be a popular appointment and wanted to get the biggest bang for the buck with an orchestrated announcement.

I was so excited I could have flown back to Syracuse without the plane.

My elation was understandable, but what surprised me was a lack of concern. I felt so confident in the **Five P's**, the **Leadership Characteristics** and the **High Performing Organization Traits** I was sure they would be as effective in a large organization as they were in the city and Syracuse. In fact, I thought with so many people engaged, it would be more effective. However, I knew the implementation wouldn't be easy since the overall Aetna culture had changed little.

I returned to the office under strict orders to keep quiet about my promotion. Only my secretary knew I had gone to Hartford. The home office would notify me two hours before the formal announcement was made to inform my staff and the other employees, so I had to sit on this for two days. When I finally got to tell them, I could barely control my emotions. I had such a close bond with every single employee that this departure was going to be the most difficult by far. I had been there longer and we had gone through more together than in any of my other positions. I took comfort in knowing my staff was so committed to our approach there was little danger of things changing much. I was proud of their development. They had embraced the concepts and become excellent practitioners.

My going away party was the biggest yet. All employees and about half of our agents attended. I had so many gifts I almost had to rent a van to get them home. There were lots of speeches, lots of laughs and lots of tears. I have never understood why more leaders don't understand **"it's all about the people"**. One of my quotes is: **"Good leaders know their numbers, Great leaders know their People"**!

I was off to Hartford!

THE BLACK KNIGHT RETURNS

The announcement of my return to the home office had the desired effect. I was well-known throughout the company and many people saw my return as a sign real change was coming. The following story was written by a group of employees in the Auto SBU:

Once upon a time in a kingdom known as Home Office, trouble was brewing. The kingdom's inhabitants had long ago lost sight of why they did what they did each day, who they were serving, and never knew if they were doing a good job or not. One thing they did know, however, was that they didn't have as many people to serve as they used to and the gold coins in the kingdom's chest were getting very low.

Despite the confusion, everyone in the kingdom kept their nose to the grindstone, but always on their own tasks. There was an air of uncertainty as everyone had a sense that it could all be for naught if the king decided one day he could get the work done elsewhere for fewer gold coins. This uncertainty caused a lot of stress and lost productivity (chatter at the water well).

There were many factors standing in the way of the kingdom's happiness and success. First, there was a huge distinction between royalty and the peasant workers. Over the years, royalty had insulated themselves from the rest of the kingdom in their cold, ostentatious castles and rarely checked on the peasants to see how they were doing.

Peasants were very intimidated by royalty and felt powerless to make a difference. They were afraid to suggest new ideas on how to perform the jobs or how to improve their work product. This was truly a shame as most peasants were very knowledgeable and sincerely wanted to increase the gold coins in the chest and be happier doing their work.

Everyone in the kingdom, including royalty, knew that

they needed to change, but had no idea how to do it or even if they could do it.

Meanwhile, in another not too distant kingdom, a knight instinctively sensed danger and heard the Home Office kingdom's cry for help. The knight quickly put on his coat of shining armor and immediately sped southeast in his black Jaguar. As he neared Home Office, the sky began to get dark, the air was heavy with apathy and discouragement. He knew he could help this kingdom as he had helped others before it.

Throwing open the tightly bolted doors, this knight in shining armor bellowed out a resounding challenge to the kingdom – "WE NEED TO CHANGE...WHAT WILL WE DO?"

This was flattering to say the least and I started to realize the high expectations my return had created. I knew, whatever we did, had to be bold and involve the entire SBU.

The CEO was pushing reengineering through the company and leaving dismay in its wake. Quick, Flexible and Right had been replaced with QFR and come to denote downsizing and layoffs. The reserves established for severance payments for laid off employees were actually called QFR reserves. What could have been a very exciting vision had morphed into something very negative and created more disdain than enthusiasm. Morale was at an all-time low, and any benefits from streamlined processes were quickly offset by lower productivity, the result of ignoring the human factor. I knew whatever we did in the Auto SBU, it was not going to be reengineering.

My staff consisted of an underwriting vice-president, a marketing vice-president, a director of human resources, a technology director, a vice-president of operations and a chief financial officer. An in-house consulting unit was attached to human resources. The marketing position was vacant.

Aetna was known for the quality of its people and I was very impressed with my staff, with one exception. The underwriting vice-president, an aggressive outspoken lady, felt she should have gotten my job, and decided to take it out on me. She was openly hostile and I knew instantly she would have to be replaced. I tried to counsel her, but she would have no part of it and asked to be re-assigned. I advised the president that we would have to find her another job. He agreed. Much to my surprise, and over my strenuous objections, they decided to send her to Syracuse as my replacement. I knew this was going to be a disaster and, unfortunately, I was right.

After a very short time, the Syracuse agents and employees were in full revolt. My phone was ringing off the hook with "how could you do this to us" calls. I pleaded with the president to make a change and when the complaints reached a fever pitch, he did. He replaced her with a capable guy who did a very good job. The office's high performance resumed much to my relief.

I now had two key positions to fill. I decided to wait on the marketing job, but had to fill the underwriting position right away. I interviewed several candidates, including the commercial underwriting director, who had led the infamous audit team back in Syracuse. Despite the CEO's resistance, based on his having no experience in automobile underwriting, I decided to give him the job. I argued underwriting is underwriting, that auto is much easier than commercial, and I needed him for his leadership ability more than his underwriting expertise. I also reminded him of our agreement. I prevailed.

My next challenge was to revamp our plan. For the prior three years, by design, our auto business had been falling, from $2.5 billion to $1.2 billion and we had withdrawn from several states. Profitability had started to improve, but it came from significant downsizing. Reversing this trend was my number one priority.

Private passenger auto, like all insurance, was regulated by the states and because it was mandated was highly political and volatile. From a regulatory standpoint, Massachusetts and New Jersey were difficult jurisdictions in which to make money, and we were trying to withdraw from both. Massachusetts was pretty much done, at a cost of $50 million. We had budgeted $120 million to get out of New Jersey. After lots of discussions and research, it became obvious to me our exit strategy for New Jersey wouldn't work. State law allowed it to bring us back if deemed necessary to increase availability for its citizens. We could pay somebody to take over our book of business and still be required to re-enter anytime the state decided to invoke the law. In addition, we had one of the leading experts on New Jersey auto managing our book and it was profitable. So I changed our New Jersey strategy from withdrawal to stay and manage.

I reviewed the changes with the president, who reluctantly agreed, but warned me the CEO would never approve. After our success in Massachusetts, he was hell-bent on getting out of New Jersey.

Accompanied by my VP for underwriting, I met the CEO in his conference room. With him were the general counsel, the corporate CFO, the head of government affairs and the president. I got into a furious argument with the CEO over our growth initiatives and the New Jersey change. I finally convinced him the growth part made sense, since shrinking to profitability was not reality. New Jersey was another story. At one point, we were both on our feet yelling at each other, and I couldn't believe I was actually doing it. I don't think anyone else in the room believed it either. I started to remind him of our agreement I could do things my way, but I didn't think this was a good time. Finally, he asked the general counsel if my interpretation of the law was correct and she said yes. He accepted the change. We left the conference room. The president called me as soon as he got back to his office and said he never thought he would see the day when I would challenge the CEO and prevail. I told him I was disappointed in his lack of support, since he didn't take part in the discussions. He apologized, and I started to realize he was on the way out.

With the plan approved, I turned my attention to transforming the SBU. We had already decided to close several branch offices and consolidate field operations into four service centers. This would generate big expense savings but would be disruptive to the business. We would have to figure out how to conduct the consolidation, minimize disruption and begin to grow all at the same time. In addition, we would have to do it with an agency pool that had all but written us off. I was starting to think bold wasn't bold enough. I described our task as the equivalent of changing a flat tire on a 747 while it's in flight. Then I remembered the armed services slogan: **"The difficult we do immediately, the impossible takes a little longer"**.

The CEO had hired consultants to implement his reengineering strategy. I didn't want them for auto, but did hire one to conduct some change management training for my staff. Our in-house consultants were very good and I knew whatever we did would have to be employee driven. In a meeting with the consultant he asked, "If you don't want to reengineer auto, what do you want to do?" I told him I wanted to build an organization that reengineers itself whenever it needs to; where continuous improvement is a way of life and not the flavor of the week; where the collective genius of every employee is focused on our mission and people are excited about working here. He said, "That's a tall order." I replied, "Yes, but we have thirty-five hundred people to do It."

I met constantly with my staff to create our new vision and come up with a name for what we were going to do. In corporate America, everything has to have a name. One of the in-house consultants came up with the vision. She said, "You have been very clear about what you want to build; an organization that produces superior results and is exciting to work in. So our new vision should be simply: **"HIGH PERFORMANCE-HIGH SATISFACTION."** I liked it and so did the rest of the team. We announced it to the company and quickly became known as the **Hi –Hi SBU**. Most importantly, our employees liked it. In no time banners and posters proclaimed a new day in Auto.

We now needed a name. We brainstormed for hours, asked for suggestions from everybody and nothing emerged. The trick was to name it and create enthusiasm around it. I had witnessed what happened to QFR and reengineering and was determined not to let that happen to us. After getting hundreds of suggestions, still nothing clicked. I was having lunch one day with the consulting team, when one of the ladies asked "What are you going to call it?" I had a sudden flash of insight. I said "That's it, we'll call it, IT." She asked what "IT" stood for. I said, absolutely nothing, it's not an acronym, it's the name.

It was a stroke of genius. As with the vision, in days banners and posters were everywhere with slogans like; "IT HAPPENS" and "AUTO DOES IT BETTER". We got the desired effect and the excitement was starting to build.

With the vision and name in place, we still had to come up with a process that would involve everyone, and start moving us toward our mission, which was to achieve an average annual growth rate of ten percent and a combined ratio of ninety-five. I sent the consulting team off to come up with a process and I turned my attention to the business. I had asked my underwriting VP and his team to identify the states with the best potential for growth in a friendly regulatory and business climate. They identified twelve and we announced an aggressive growth initiative for each.

I hit the road visiting some of our key agents in each state telling the story of the new SBU. I got a call from one of the general managers saying his largest agent with a ten million dollar book of business was threatening to move it and he needed me to come down and talk them out of it. I arrived at the meeting and decided to listen to their complaints before I talked about the new things we were doing. They had a long list including reduced commissions, reduced profit sharing, reduced capacity to write new business and very poor service. When they finished, I told them I knew everything they said was true, and in their situation, I would have moved the business two years ago. Then I said, "After enduring all that pain, I can't imagine why you would leave now when things are getting so much better." They were a bit surprised at my response, but listened intently to the changes we were making. After a lengthy discussion, I asked them to give us a year and if we failed to deliver, I would pay the expenses for them to move their book. I also asked them to call me direct if at any time we failed to deliver. They agreed.

We decided to organize the service centers into self-managed teams. The details were still being developed, but the structure was set. When we closed the branch offices we offered transfers to any employees who wanted to move, but this still left a significant need for new hires. Service was going to be the hallmark of the new service centers so we took this opportunity to diversify the staff to promote this idea. We figured it was relatively easy to teach people the technical side of insurance so we hired people from service industries like retail, healthcare, teaching and hospitality. The mix was magical and we were able to improve service levels throughout the consolidation, unheard of in our business.

I decided it was time to fill the marketing position and asked my human resources head to compile a list of candidates. I interviewed several but no one stood out. Then my underwriting VP suggested a bond manager for Aetna in Richmond we both knew, praised for his agency management skills. I interviewed him and offered him the job. He accepted, and we now had three Richmond natives in key positions. We soon became known as the three amigos from Virginia.

The consulting team developed a process for "IT" and we called a meeting of all key players for their presentation. They proposed an announcement of the launch of "IT" that reiterated our Vision and Mission and the need to restructure to achieve it. As long as it contributed to moving closer to that goal everything was on the table. No sacred cows and no idea would be dismissed without a thorough vetting. We would ask all employees to form teams of ten to twenty members, as appropriate and imagine everything a High Performing/High Satisfaction organization would need to achieve its mission. No template would be provided; everyone could contribute.

The stories would be submitted to the consulting team who would organize a diverse team to review the stories and compile a list of common themes. With themes identified, we would put together another team to develop for each an implementation plan. During the process teams would report findings to, and solicit feedback from, the entire organization. I thought it was brilliant and knew that "IT" was going to happen!

The employee benefits division had adopted a self-managed team approach a year earlier and had implemented this structure in several of its operations. A friend from my first home office tour was a team leader. I called and invited her to lunch. We had stayed in touch over the years and she accepted. I shared with her what we were doing in Auto and told her that I could really use her help and asked if she would consider coming to work for me. Her initial reaction was to decline. She knew nothing about the property and casualty business having spent her entire career in employee benefits and she was doing quite well where she was. I said I needed her for her self-managed team knowledge not her business knowledge and wouldn't you like to be a part of something as exciting as transforming a $1.2 billion business that is likely to become the most successful SBU in the company? She asked if I truly believed that and I said absolutely. I also told her I would make it worth her while financially and probably move up her retirement by five years. I invited her to spend some time with the consulting team to be fully briefed on what we were doing. She reluctantly agreed. I briefed the team on what I wanted to do and they were all for it. My friend came and was convinced to join us. This would prove to be a critical ingredient in our implementation.

The stories started coming in and the creativity of the people was on full display. We got stories written as fairy tales, as news reports, as competitive analysis, as magazine articles, and as a constitution for example.

The following is one example:

The CONSTITUTION Of The Personal Auto SBU

PREAMBLE
We, the members of Team 7, in order to form a more perfect organization, establish justice, ensure employee tranquility, promote the benefits of High Performance/High Satisfaction through teamwork for ourselves and our customers, do ordain and establish the CONSTITUTION for the personal Auto SBU.

BILL OF RIGHTS

We hold these truths to be self-evident, that all employees are created equal and are endowed with certain inalienable rights. Among these are:

- Freedom to EXPRESS oneself without fear of criticism or retribution.

- Freedom to be treated with RESPECT.

- Freedom to be CREATIVE, INNOVATIVE AND IMAGINATIVE.

- Freedom to be RECOGNIZED for one's contributions.

- Freedom to DEVELOP oneself and ACHIEVE self-actualization.

- Freedom to PURSUE career and development OPPORTUNITIES.

- Freedom for all employees to be treated in a FAIR and EQUITABLE manner.

- Freedom to receive ongoing input and FEEDBACK on one's performance.

PETITION OF EXPECTATIONS

To ensure that all employees have the opportunity to reach their maximum potential, we hold that the following expectations MUST become an integral part of the Personal Auto SBU for all employees.

- The right to participate in the DECISION-MAKING PROCESS.

- The right to work in an environment with OPEN COMMUNICATION where information and resources are SHARED.

- The right to a REWARD system that RECOGNIZES and PAYS FOR PERFORMANCE.

- The right to be EMPOWERED to implement SBU strategy through self-direction.

- The right to participate in CROSS-FUNCTIONAL activities, projects and training.

- The right to a more EXPEDIENT DECISION-MAKING PROCESS through a reduction in the number of referral and approval levels.

- The right to profit through GAINSHARING when the SBU is profitable.

- The right to an INTEGRATED COMPUTER ACCESS system which provides a user-friendly interface to all automated files.

- The right to OUTSOURCE for the best technology, goods and services available.

- The right to participate in OPEN COMPETITION/OPEN POSTING FOR PROJECTS to increase opportunities.

- The right to expect ACCOUNTABILITY from ALL employees – responsibility means accountability.

- The right to participate in the EVALUATION of those with whom one works, i.e., co-workers, team leaders, and other *project leaders in order to improve overall performance throughout the SBU.*

BILL OF PARTICULARS

To achieve and ensure the rights and expectations set forth in this Constitution, there must be fundamental changes in both organizational CULTURE and STRUCTURE. CULTURAL change will involve a personal commitment from each individual to pursue the rights and expectations of all employees. STRUCTURAL change, however, will by design, ensure that those rights and expectations are realized. The STRUCTURE will reinforce the new CULTURE.

TO ACHIEVE THESE GOALS, LET IT BE PUT FORTH
THAT THE PERSONAL AUTO SBU WILL BE ORGANIZED INTO A

TEAM ENVIRONMENT

TEAMS WILL CONSIST OF THE FOLLOWING CHARACTERISTICS

- **SELF-MANAGED/SELF-DIRECTED**

- **PROCESS-DRIVEN AS OPPOSED TO FUNCTION-DRIVEN**

- **CROSS FUNCTIONAL RESPONSIBILITIES FOR TEAM MEMBERS**

- **CUSTOMER FOCUSED**

- **HIGH PERFORMANCE/HIGH SATISFACTION**

WRIT OF ASSISTANCE

Whereas Team 7 has put forth a new CONSTITUTION for the Personal Auto SBU establishing the character and conception of its workplace, laying the basic principles to which its internal life is to be conformed, organizing employee working relationships, distributing the functions of its different internal parts, and prescribing the manner of the exercise of teamwork, and

Whereas through the PREAMBLE to this Constitution has set forth the reasons for its enactment and the objects sought to be accomplished; and

Whereas it proposes recognition of an employee BILL OF RIGHTS as fundamental to a High Performance/High Satisfaction business organization; and

Whereas realized EXPECTATIONS as petitioned for, fairly administered to all employees, is seen as a necessary, integral part of successful, maximum achievement;

We therefore, respectfully pray for a grant of Assistance through fair, dedicated evaluation of these PARTICULARS for **"change."**

I was impressed with the stories and more convinced than ever we had all the answers we needed. The consulting team organized a very diverse group to review the stories and identify the common themes. This group came up with twelve major themes. We then formed twelve teams, one to deal with each theme, and charged them with developing the specifications and implementation plan for each. This was a major part of "IT" and each team was to continue to get input from the entire organization.

My wife went back to work for Aetna soon after we returned. We had settled in a nice community in Farmington and hired a nanny to take care of Nicky. Since we both traveled, we hired a very mature nanny. It didn't work out and after two months we were looking for a replacement. In the interim, we put Nicky in day-care. There was an eighteen year old, Katy, working in the day-care center and approached my wife and said she would like to come to work for us as a nanny. My wife told her that since we both traveled, sometimes overnight, we were looking for somebody a bit more mature. The next day Katy approached her again and said she was very mature for her age and very responsible, she had gotten to know Nicky and knew she could do a good job for us. She then handed her a binder. When she got home, we reviewed the binder. Katy had included her resume', her educational background, her family history, references, and a complete plan for how she would care for Nicky. She also suggested that we talk to her parents. We were blown away. This was undoubtedly the most comprehensive application for a job that I had seen and from an eighteen year old. She was practicing **the Five P's** and I was certain hadn't heard of them. We talked to Katy's parents who assured us she was the most responsible eighteen year old on the planet, had always been mature beyond her years, had fallen in love with Nicky, and would take excellent care of him. Her mother also promised to be back-up on the nights we were out of town. We hired her; she worked for us for almost five years and took excellent care of our son.

Shortly after arriving in Hartford I held my first all-employee meeting. Aetna had an internal broadcast system which allowed us to reach every field office in the country. Business head speeches were always covered by our PR department. The following article appeared in the company magazine following my speech.

"Auto on road to profitability"
<u>No pain, no gain</u>

About three years ago, the Personal Auto SBU began pursuing a shrink-and-become-profitable strategy that at first produced nothing but pain. Premiums dropped from $2.5 billion in 1990 to $1.2 billion in 1992. More than 1 million customers were forced to buy their auto insurance from other companies as Aetna withdrew from almost 30 states. Hundreds of employees lost their jobs as 20 personal lines branch offices were consolidated in four high-tech Auto Homeowner Business Centers.

But, the pain recently has turned to gain. Personal Auto reemerged in1992 as one of Aetna's most profitable property-casualty businesses.

Personal Auto posted a loss of $61 million in 1991, which included a $55 million charge to exit Massachusetts. But in 1992 the SBU earned $27 million in what was generally a poor year for the industry.

On Jan. 14, Alfred L. Austin was brought in from Syracuse to be the new SBU Head. It's up to Austin to continue the turn around. No new-comer to Aetna, Austin has been with the company for 22 years, most of them in the field. On March 18, he held his first meeting with Auto's home office staff to outline his hopes and expectations for the SBU over the coming years.

With an informal and easygoing speaking style, Austin took advantage of his departmental debut to give his audience a glimpse of his business philosophy. Austin said four keys to success that he used in Syracuse, and that Auto must pursue, are: a tenacious approach to employee development, a fanatical approach to customer service, a dogged approach to account selection and an unwavering commitment to agents.

He also revealed his love for his job, "If I won the lotto tomorrow, I would not resign. I love what I'm doing."

In general, Austin said he wanted the Personal Auto SBU to be a "world-class organization, one that is extremely customer-sensitive, easy for agents to do business with and extremely profitable. I'm not sure that 15 percent return on equity is enough. What's wrong with 20 percent or 30 percent?" he asked.

Austin is a self-proclaimed fanatic when it comes to customer service. "Everyone talks about superior customer service. It's like motherhood and apple pie; no one's against superior customer service. But you know, few companies have been able to make it come to life."

"Achieving superior customer service depends on attitudinal change. Even if you're processing hundreds of bills a day, you have to keep in mind that every one of those bills eventually is going to a person just like you," he said.

Can Austin continue the momentum and maybe even reach his dream of seeing auto become "extremely profitable?" Before you dismiss his mention of a 30 percent ROE as speaker's hyperbole, take a look at his record in Syracuse.

During his six and a half years in Syracuse, revenues increased from $19 million to $85 million, and profits went from $300,000 to $9.2 million.

Terry D'Italia

Following my speech the PR person approached me and said, "Mr. Austin, you don't give speeches, you give sermons." I said, "It's in my genes, my father was a Baptist minister." Then he said, "You believe people can move mountains, don't you?" I said, "I know they can, I've seen them do it."

Things were happening fast. We had so many projects going it was difficult to keep track. Fortunately, I had the best executive assistant in the company, who was always on top of things and made sure I got accomplished what I needed to do and on schedule. I relied on her a lot and she never failed to deliver.

When the underwriting VP did his state analysis, he also looked at areas where we were experiencing significant losses. One of those areas was down-state New York. The analysis showed the quality of our book was good and our rates were generally equal to or higher than our major competitors. So the only other variable was claim payments. I approached the head of claim, shared our findings and asked if he could isolate our problem. He refused, stating he had full confidence there was no issue with claim. But he had no benchmark absent competitive information about claim settlements, so it was difficult to compare our results with our competitors. Internally we tracked average paid amounts, not as a performance measure, but for information. It was not a precise measure, but with large numbers a good indicator of how payments were moving.

We discussed this issue in detail at one of my staff meetings. We wrote a lot of business in down-state New York and could not ignore the problem, so we brainstormed about how we could get information to convince the claim department to take action. One of the consultants said, "We should hire a firm to conduct a survey of our top five competitors and use their average paid amounts for comparison" Another said, "They might participate if we could guarantee the survey was anonymous and all would share the results." We used this approach, convinced all five to participate and learned our down-state New York average paid amounts were 30 percent higher than the average and 40 percent higher than the lowest competitor. I knew the head of claim would discount this stunning news, because he knew that kind of information did not exist. I called the head of the down-state claim service center. He was a young, ambitious, up and comer and had sought my council on occasion. I called him direct, shared the results of the report, cautioned him against discussing this with his boss, and told him this was an opportunity for him to take the initiative, correct this situation and emerge a hero. He jumped at the chance, and in a very short time corrected the situation and significantly improved the profit picture in down-state.

Shortly after I took over the Auto SBU, another man was named head of the Homeowners SBU. I knew him, but not well. Homeowner was a much smaller business and closely aligned with Auto. The service centers would handle both so he and I were attached at the hip. He was as left brained as I was right and, we complimented each other extremely well. Once we figured this out, we became a strong team and were often identified as an example of the teamwork needed throughout the company. He was a supportive partner and played a key role throughout the implementation of "IT".

The theme teams were hard at work. The service centers were progressing as planned and the sting of the lay-offs was more than off-set by the excitement of "IT" and the achievement of a Hi/Hi vision. We had managed to do what the CEO had failed to accomplish with Quick, Flexible and Right. There was so much excitement in the Auto SBU people were lining up to come to work there. We were changing everything; the structure, products, technology, compensation, training, authority levels and how we serviced our agents. Some of the technology required for our integrated systems approach had literally not been invented. We teamed up with IBM to create it. Now if that's not cutting edge, what is?

In the fall of 1993 my first mentor and boss in Newark retired at the age of 52. I knew from my plan meeting with the CEO he was on the way out, so I was not surprised. More than my first mentor, he had helped me throughout my entire career and was a close confidant and friend. I would miss him.

His successor was completely unknown to people in the property and casualty division. He had been in charge of Aetna International and identified as one of the contenders for CEO. His charge was to fix the rest of P & C, and since I had become the face of change, the CEO asked me to introduce him to P & C employees. In a company-wide broadcast, I gave some information on his background, and followed with a talk-show style question and answer period, including those from the field offices via pre-arranged phone lines. From that day on, I developed a very close working relationship with him. He knew what was going on in the Auto SBU and was certain it had some application to the rest of P & C. I assured him it did.

Organization of the home office was hotly debated. We were well on the way with self-managed teams in the service centers but as yet had no definitive agreement on Hartford. The field said self-managed teams were too effective not to have them everywhere. We had more meetings over this and the elimination of offices than any other "IT" issue. After numerous meetings and no decision, I said we should appoint a three-person team to collect and analyze the data and make a recommendation to the group. The group, although some with reluctance, agreed to accept that option. After a week of study the three-person group recommended a self-managed team structure for the home office; cubicles would replace offices. I was impressed that, after all the raw emotion and vigorous debates, with strong feelings on both sides, once this decision was announced, everybody got on board. There were no water-cooler or hallway after-debates or complaining. That was a healthy sign that Hi/Hi was happening!

I was interviewed by our PR department shortly after the home office change was announced. The reporter commented the elimination of offices was a big symbolic move and likely to send shock-waves through-out the company. I told him it had nothing to do with symbolism, but everything to do with **communications**. For years officers had boasted of having an "open door policy," so not having doors was certain to be better.

One day I got a call from Frank Zizzamia. He was in the I T department, not to be confused with "IT", and wanted to discuss a project he was working on that he thought could be useful to the Auto business. I agreed to meet. Frank had developed a software program to score auto risks and identify those with the best profit potential. Most states had assigned risk pools to accommodate riskier drivers who had difficulty finding coverage in the standard market. All companies licensed in the state had to accept a certain number of these drivers, based on their market share. Frank's program would enable us to pick the best of the worst. Frank needed a home to test his program and get funding for the continued development. After consultation with my technology team, we agreed to give Frank a home. As it turned out, this was the beginning of a system known as predictive analytics. Frank was on the leading edge. This concept would go on to be the underwriting model for personal lines and small commercial accounts used by all insurers. It is the true manifestations of the law of large numbers. At its core, it says there is no such thing as bad accounts, just bad prices and if you can price your business correctly, you can make money. Frank would go on to become one of the leading experts in this field.

When I arrived in Hartford I got involved in the Urban League's Black Executive Exchange Program and through them was invited to give the keynote speech at Grambling University's fall business conference. The conference was comprised of the faculty and students enrolled in the business school, roughly five hundred individuals. I was introduced at the conference by the president of the university. After reviewing my background, he said to the audience, "Now Mr. Austin is going to tell us about the struggle for minorities in corporate America." After my greeting, I said, "With all due respect to the president, I'm not here to tell you anything about struggling. In fact, if you think working in corporate America is a struggle, you should try something else. I'm here to tell you about the tremendous opportunities in corporate America and how you can take advantage of them." I then went through a meticulous explanation of the **Five P's** and the rules of engagement. I told them while assimilation was not necessary, conforming to certain cultural norms was. A corporate dress code is not an affront to your right to choose, but a requirement for all employees, that represents the values of a particular company and how they want to be perceived. Enjoying what you do is absolutely critical to the passion required to excel, whatever your job. Then I shared with them more of my background, going from the farm to the executive suite and enjoying every minute of it. I got a standing ovation.

Following the speech I held a workshop with the faculty that was contentious and lively. I told them they should be careful about misleading students. While it may be difficult to succeed, it was difficult for everybody, and performance, not skin color, was going to be the determining factor. True, discrimination was still alive and well, but it was now the exception rather than the rule. They accused me of being naïve and I was never invited back.

We ended 1993 with eight percent growth and a combined ratio of 97%. We earned $129 million. It was the first time Auto had grown in four years. We held a massive celebration. Even the CEO joined in, but cautioned against growing too fast in the wrong places. I assured him we were well aware of the components of "profitable growth." The claim manager in downstate New York had stepped up and results were improving at a rapid pace. New York was such a big part of our book, in any given year it could make or break us. New Jersey remained profitable, but the CEO still harbored a desire to withdraw. To his credit, he didn't pressure me.

The following article appeared in the company newsletter:

Auto SBU looks to continue impressive turnaround

A new, streamlined business strategy, a completely redesigned field office structure, and an evolving culture that replaces hierarchical management with self-managed teams has been the formula for success in the Personal Auto SBU.

"We've got a lot of good things going on," says SBU head Al Austin. "We still have a long way to go, but we're pretty optimistic that the improvement will continue."

Despite a competitive and politically volatile regulatory environment, Auto's operating earnings have increased in each of the last three years, reaching $129 million in 1993. In between, however, Aetna had to make some difficult decisions.

The first was a fundamental one. Should the company stay in the personal auto insurance business at all? Claim losses were high, and profits were low. The auto markets in many states were no more than black holes that continued to swallow Aetna's money.

A new culture

But the story of Auto's turn-around is as much about culture change as it is about new marketing strategies. The SBU completely reengineered its field organization, centralizing operations into four business centers – Syracuse, N.Y., Fall River, Mass., Tampa, Fla., and Houston.

Gone is the former supervisor-manager structure. In its place are self-managed teams with the authority and the technological tools to provide more focused and more responsive customer service – at reduced cost. Once complete, the transition to business centers will reduce Personal Auto's field expenses by 50 percent.

Changes are being made in Hartford too. "We're also trying to change the culture of the home office to make it more like the field," Austin said. "We want to break down the traditional walls between functions and departments. And we're looking at every single process, trying to squeeze out anything that doesn't add value."

Part of the change has involved downsizing, and staff reductions have been taking place in the SBU over the past 18 months. Austin admits they have affected morale, but feels the cultural changes have helped soften the blow.

"It's obviously had an effect, but I think we've done a pretty good job managing it," he says. "The morale in our business centers, for example, is higher than it's ever been. People are very excited about potential for cultural change here."

Much of that change has been driven from the bottom up by employee suggestions. Austin estimates that 85 percent of the SBU's employees have been involved in its cultural transformation.

We've got to perform

Aetna is committed to staying in the private passenger auto insurance market, but nothing is guaranteed, Austin knows. "We've got to perform and meet financial standards if we're going to stay in this business," he says. "We accept that. That's the way it should be."

I think the auto business has a lot of potential," says Austin. "We expect our improvement to continue, because we're not there yet. We still have a lot to do, but we're well on our way. I like our chances."

Walt Cherniak

My staff had done an incredible job. I found they were as committed to Theory Y as I was but needed someone leading to allow them to practice it. **High Performance/High Satisfaction** was a reality and we were reaping the benefits. Mike Hammer even called our transformation the most successful reengineering effort of the 90's, even though we never called it that. I was listed in the Who's Who Registry of Business Leaders. Life was good.

During the first quarter of 1994, I got a call from our public relations department, asking if I would agree to be interviewed by BusinessWeek. They were doing an article on the Private Passenger Auto market and wanted to get our perspective.

I agreed and the interview was scheduled. The PR guys came over to prep me for the interview. They said that typically the magazine would interview several people for an article like this and may not use anything from the interview. Since it was going to be a positive article, my job was to get the company's name mentioned at least once. To help with that, it was important for me to establish a good rapport with the reporter. They had researched him and found he was a baseball fanatic, so I should try to impress him with my baseball knowledge. I said that's going to be a problem, since I am not a fan and know absolutely nothing about baseball. I could see the panic in their faces. Then they suggested I spend the next two days becoming a baseball expert. I said, "That's not going to happen. I doubt if I could and I'm not going to risk coming off as an idiot, trying to appear to be an expert in something I know nothing about." They feared this golden opportunity would slip through their fingers and there was nothing they could do.

The day of the interview the reporter arrived in my office with his assistant and two people from our PR department. I had my office decorated with several model cars, including a number of Jaguar models. He immediately started talking about my collection and asking questions about each model and wanted to know if I drove a Jaguar. I answered his questions and told him I drove a 1988 Jaguar XJS 12 cylinder that was black with tan interior. He was impressed. It turned out his father was a car fanatic and a big Jaguar fan; he had grown up around cars. My PR guys were beside themselves with joy. The interview lasted about two hours and when the reporter left I felt we would at least get the Aetna name mentioned once.

Two days later, the PR guy called me nearly out of breath. The reporter had called to ask if I would pose for a picture with my Jaguar in front of Aetna's home office, to accompany his article. When I hesitated, he said, "You don't understand, this is big, we were hoping to get Aetna's name mentioned once and now we have the opportunity to have you and the home office featured in the article!" I agreed, after all it was my chance for my fifteen seconds of fame.

I couldn't believe what went into this picture. A film crew, complete with make-up artist came up from New York. They spent three hours and took over seven hundred pictures, to get the right one.

The article with my picture appeared in the April 4, 1994 edition of Businessweek, with a quote from me and Aetna's name mentioned several times. **"Honesty is the best policy."** I got hundreds of emails and letters from all over the country from Aetna employees and customers. The employees' e-mails said it was great to see the company associated with something positive and it was sure to help business. The customers' emails and letters were mixed. Some wanted to know who insured my car since Aetna had cancelled coverage on their sports cars.

The business was going really well. I spent a lot of time visiting agents and in the service centers. Traveling on one of the corporate jets was a lot more convenient than commercial travel and I was enjoying it. The atmosphere in the service centers and in home office resembled Syracuse, another indication that "IT" accomplished its goals.

The new president was trying to change the whole division and having some success. He had even adopted our mission of growth and a 95% combined ratio, which two years prior, the CEO had called ridiculous. We still had issues with claim. After our study, other SBU's started to question their effectiveness and called for more financial discipline around the payout amounts. The president had a financial background and was also having a problem with an operation that paid out between four and five billion dollars a year, with no idea if it was the correct amount. I tried to work with the head of claim to get him to change his position, but he would not bulge. He saw claims as a customer service organization and the amounts they paid out were irrelevant.

By the end of summer, the head of claim retired. We immediately launched a search for his replacement and hired one of the leading executive search firms in the country. We created a profile of the ideal candidate, a hybrid of claim executives that included someone with a working knowledge of claims, and strong overall business acumen. I was on the search committee along with several of my colleagues. For three months we interviewed twenty plus candidates from all over the country and could not find a suitable person.

Then one day the CEO's secretary called, saying he wanted me to meet with him and the president. When I arrived, the CEO said, "Al you know we have searched the country for someone to run claims with no success. You have always been the internal benchmark for this position. Since we have been unable to find someone who measured up, I have no choice but to ask you to take the job." I said, "While I'm flattered, my work in the Auto SBU is not done and I'm having too much fun to leave now." He agreed my work wasn't finished but thought my continued involvement wasn't critical to its progress. I couldn't disagree. The changes we made were so massive and the results so good, there was little danger anyone would try to reverse anything. Then he said, "You'll still be right here, able to keep an eye on things, and involved with the president, in running the whole show." I accepted the claim job.

My staff was sorry to see me go, but not overly concerned. They knew that we had reached the "point of no return," and with or without me, they were going to continue the progress. I was pleased and proud of what we had accomplished, and felt confident it would continue.

THE PRODIGAL SON RETURNS

The announcement of my return to claims created a lot of excitement. It was rumored that no one in the history of the company had gone from claim representative to the head of the department without holding any interim positions. The expectations of the employees were high. I knew most claim employees felt their approach to claim handling was outdated and needed serious changes. This also gave me a high degree of confidence we could move quickly to improve the operation. Working with the SBU heads and others, the new president started developing some of the plans for the transformation and my return was rumored for several months. So, things were positioned for me to hit the ground running.

I was introduced to the department by the president and one of the operations VP from claim using the same format we used to introduce the president. In my remarks and answers to questions, I told employees I expected every single person to be involved in coming up with the solutions we needed to implement. Everything was on the table. I promised them we would do anything, as long as it was moral and legal, to reduce our payouts and improve customer service. I also said; **"We're going to stop paying employees for blindly following guidelines and start paying them for making good business decisions."** Then I promised to visit all twenty-three service centers in the next ninety days and asked them to share their ideas with me directly.

The claim department's issues were very different than Auto. While the organization would benefit from some changes, the biggest problems were with the processes and procedures used to conduct investigations and settlements and the performance measures used to evaluate results. Driving some of this was that old question about who was the customer. The position of the prior head of claims was that all claimants, first party or third, were customers. So one of my first pronouncements was that was going to change and we were going to adopt the approach we used, very successfully, in Syracuse; a bifurcated approach where first party claimants were treated as customers and third party claimants were treated fairly and equitably, but questionable situations would be resolved in favor of the company. Any spike in defense cost would be temporary and more than off-set by savings in payouts.

  The department was notorious for its standards of performance contained in a three ring binder, three inches thick. It laid out exactly what every claim rep had to do in every case, with no room for discretion. Audit teams would use the standards to evaluate the appropriateness of file handling during their reviews, so no matter how serious or minor a case was, the claim rep was required to follow the standards and failure to do so would result in a reprimand. We had a ceremonial burning of the standards at my first staff meeting and I instructed everyone from this day forward to trust the claim rep to decide what needed to be done on each file, based on the circumstances of the case. We also established a team to develop a simplified claim handling process for small claims to take them out of the main workflow and have them handled by a team with a minimal, automated process. With the level of reviews during the life of a case, there was little chance anything necessary would be missed.

  One of the other issues was a performance measure to control the number of outstanding cases. In addition to case reserves, the actuaries would add supplemental reserves based partially on the number of out-standings, so the claim department would take extraordinary measures to close files. This included settlement days where plaintiff attorneys would be invited into the office and claim reps would try to persuade them to settle cases, which usually meant paying more than the case was worth. Since the amount they paid was not subject to scrutiny, this was an unintended consequence of little concern to the claim rep or the management. I immediately removed out-standings as a performance measure. We would continue to track them, but would not react if they were elevated. Part of the rationale I gave my staff was our past practices eliminated the biggest leverage we had. We had billions of dollars and invested the reserves. The plaintiff attorneys couldn't afford to sit on a case as long as we could, because they had to pay the bills. I also knew, from my Syracuse experience, any spike in out-standings would be temporary because as soon as the plaintiff attorneys figured out our new strategy, they would settle cases for the right amount, which we were always willing to pay. I met with the actuaries to explain our new approach so they wouldn't panic when they saw the spike.

Finally, re-integrating claim back into the mainstream of the business presented some issues because in most cases they were not co-located with the SBU's. We would have to come up with some interim measures and a longer term approach that brought the organization back together.

My staff was a bit nervous about these changes, but I was adamant. This was exactly the approach we used in Syracuse and it was the major contributing factor to our profitability. We also developed a vision for claims. It was the Five F's: **"Build an organization that was Fast, Focused, Flexible Frugal and Fun."** They gradually came around.

The following article appeared in the company newsletter shortly after my announcement.

Claim must simplify, change culture to regain pre-eminence in industry

The claim operation of the property-casualty group must simplify its processes and revamp its culture if it is to regain its former status as the best claim operation in the business, according to unit leader Al Austin.

Austin spoke Nov. 16 to claim employees in Hartford, striding around among members of the audience in the home office auditorium, challenging them with questions and offering his view of what Claim must do to be successful. He told the group they must become "coaches, counselors and barrier-busters" for their customers and employees and shed their role as "policemen" who enforce outdated rules and processes.

"We can't develop the right solutions until we truly understand the problems," Austin said. "In the past, we've often treated the symptoms without ever recognizing and treating the disease. So the symptoms just kept coming back."

Austin said reengineering is about improving productivity. Gains in productivity come by changing processes, eliminating unnecessary work and maximizing the use of technology.

"We have to look at our underlying processes. You can't just automate work; you have to try to eliminate it first," he said. Austin told a story about a feedback form that had been sent to Auto customers for years. To administer it, there was a large team and an elaborate process. Auto discovered that no one found the form useful. They eliminated it and saved $4.5 million. They went on to eliminate eight more forms, saving millions more.

"Not only were these forms costly, they slowed down the process of getting the job done and added no value. So, we saved money, but we also made the process much more efficient for our people," he said.

Claim will need to improve its customer service, Austin said, because it is the sole sustainable competitive advantage a company has. "Any competitor with a photocopier can duplicate our products, and anyone with a calculator can compete with our rates. The only thing they can't duplicate is our customer service."

"Customer service is not what we do; it's how we do it."

"Figuring out the best way to do all the things we're talking about will require a cultural transformation," Austin said. "A group of managers sitting at a table won't come up with all the answers. We need to involve front-line people in deciding what goes, what stays and how we do what stays more efficiently. The goal is to have the most knowledgeable and free-thinking people involved in every decision."

Austin said his goal was to have a Claim culture that "harnesses the collective genius of the entire organization." He said that will require leaders who are willing to solicit, involve, and listen to the people in the organization, and it will require a goal that transcends the boundaries of Claim.

Austin expressed his belief that Aetna still has the best people in the industry. "I have complete confidence that the people in this organization can and will build a world-class claim department that is second to none in every respect," he said.

"We have to work as a team," Austin said, "We have to do whatever possible to make P-C successful. So, if you see something wrong, speak up. Act like an owner."

Ernest Mills

I started my service center visits and was overjoyed at what I found. I was greeted by enthusiastic employees who had completely embraced our new strategy. I was met with skits, songs, time capsules and all manner of ways expressing the new approach. I made it a point at each center to get ideas and implement them on the spot. I was in California, at an all-employee meeting, talking about the standards of performance, when a very experienced claim rep said, "Mr. Austin I am so happy to see those go, because they were time consuming and in most cases added nothing to the process. " Then he told me one of the standards for auto accidents was the file must contain a picture of the scene, even if there were no questions about liability and the accident happened in some remote section of highway. "So I would have to drive thirty miles to take a picture of a section of highway that meant absolutely nothing." I said, "I hope you didn't do that very often." He said, "I didn't. I took several pictures of different sections of highways, kept them in my desk and when I needed one, stuck it in the file." I applauded him and thanked him for his ingenuity and said that it was thoughtful, innovative people like him that had kept the company afloat. I also said to the group that no one should ever again do anything that would not assist in their effective handling of a file; just put a note in the file that "Al said I didn't have to get a picture."

This was typical of the feedback I got during every visit. By the time I finished my initial tour the standards of performance were officially buried.

Measuring customer satisfaction was always tricky in claims. While we had resolved who the customer was, how satisfied you wanted them to be became the issue. As I learned back in Richmond, inflating claim values is one thing most otherwise law-abiding citizens, feel totally justified in doing. When I arrived in claim, the objective was to have a ninety-five percent customer satisfaction rating. I said to my staff, "If ninety-five percent of our claimants are satisfied, we're paying too much to settle claims." Unfortunately, I didn't know what the magic number was, but after much debate, we settled on seventy-five. The president and the SBU heads were a little concerned about this, but after a thorough explanation, they agreed. I also assured them if justified complaints rose, we would adjust our thinking.

Re-integrating claim into the overall business process was problematic because most had been moved to different locations. We put together a plan to move them back together as leases expired. In the interim, we required general managers, SBU managers and claim managers to hold periodic meetings and participate in each other's planning process. Since everyone recognized the importance of this, the interim solution worked very well.

The remaining issue to address was the control of payout amounts and how to insure we avoided another downstate New York situation. We hired the same consultant we used in auto, with the same rules to do a more expansive survey. This was helpful, but was a point-in-time view that had limited value on an ongoing basis. The survey results were mixed. In some areas we were average or better, but the inconsistency highlighted the need for a more systematic approach. As luck would have it, a software company in Texas was just launching a system that claimed to assist the claim rep in arriving at the prevailing settlement amount for every possible injury in every jurisdiction in the country, and provide management information on how our settlements stacked up. I was contacted about a presentation. They had sold two systems at that point and the implementation was too early to have much feedback. The system was called Colossus and the company claimed it would revolutionize claim handling. The price tag was nearly fifteen million dollars

   I agreed to meet. I had had good experience with leading edge technology both with the predictive analytics for assigned risk take-out for New York and our work with IBM to create the software to run our integrated systems for the service centers. Therefore, I was not deterred by the newness of the system.

The presentation was impressive and we agreed to a rather involved test. The results were even more impressive and I was sold. We had learned from the other two implementations claim reps feared the system would replace them. This was a common theme during this time, with the rapid expansion of technology and the resulting downsizing everywhere. I made a note we would have to figure out how to address this upfront.

Now that I was sold, I had to sell the CEO, the President and the SBU heads, since they would have to pay for this. To get approval for a $15 million check, I knew I was going to have to show the direct benefit to each SBU. Our test results had shown we had a significant opportunity for savings, somewhere between $500 and $750 million. So I told the group I would commit to saving $500 million the first year, showing what that impact would have on each SBU, allowing them to include a line item in their plan for claim savings. This would not only be a big boast to their profit potential, but would also create the link to re-integrate claims into the business. Having a shared objective was a sure way to create the lines of communications necessary to promote the teamwork we were trying to develop among the units. I offered to resign if we failed to deliver. They agreed to buy the system.

A significant amount of calibration was necessary to implement the system, so I decided to form a team of claim reps with at least two people from each service center to handle it. I would have them be ambassadors for Colossus when they returned. I also announced the implementation with a direct broadcast to all service centers. I first described the system, shared with them what we were trying to achieve and assured them there was no expectation of staff reductions associated with Colossus. Since trust was never an issue, people accepted this. Then I told them **I believed the right technology in the hands of an engaged workforce, was a powerful tool and we were going to use that**

tool to grow the business, not shrink it.

The implementation was flawless. I was reminded again, **"You can get people to do almost anything if your motives are pure, your rationale convincing and sincere and the interaction takes place in an atmosphere of trust and mutual respect."** The company asked if we would assist them in other implementations. I declined, but told them they were free to use our process. He said, "But your team is the process." I reminded him we already had jobs.

We were moving fast and reviewing or changing just about everything. The president made it clear, and I knew, we didn't have years, but months to achieve the high performance necessary for P & C to reach its financial goals.

During this same time, we were embroiled in two massive national issues; asbestos and environmental liability. We insured several clients involved in both and were trying to get a handle on our exposure for years of coverage, but had major questions about whether or not it applied for environmental liability losses. Environmental losses resulted from chemicals seeping into the ground over a number of years. Our policies were intended to cover sudden and accidental losses. The legal battle over this issue would cost the industry hundreds of millions of dollars and expose it to billions if coverage was invoked. We had a separate unit set up to deal only with this issue. In the summer of 1995, rumors spread Aetna was considering some form of restructuring to raise money to fund its environmental liability exposure, and increase capital to support its three major divisions. They ran the gamut from a sale of the P & C operation, a total spin-off, a partial spin-off, to borrowing the money. It wouldn't take long before this issue was settled.

The board of directors hired a major consulting firm to advise it on the best strategy going forward. Since Aetna had two very large businesses, P & C and Health-care, and one smaller business in the International operation, it had several choices.

Things were progressing quite well. Morale improved significantly, the standards of performance were a distance memory, a team structure was in place, and Colossus was ahead of schedule in delivering the $500 million savings promised to the businesses. Unfortunately rumors of a pending sale of the P & C division were rampant and required a significant amount of energy to keep people focused on the job at hand.

    I decided to hold a two-day management retreat in Arizona to celebrate our success to date and make sure we stayed on track for our continued progress. The message for the meeting was that despite what the board might decide to do, our mission, to build a world-class claim department, had not changed. In the event of a spin-off our performance would be more critical than ever and in the event of a sale, the buyer would be paying for a world-class operation and it was up to us to deliver. We were not victims, but critical ingredients in a major transaction that might result in a different name on the door, but would require no less from us. I closed the meeting with Invictus by William Ernest Henley:

> **Out of the night that covers me,**
> **Black as a pit from pole to pole,**
> **I thank whatever gods may be**
> **For my unconquerable soul.**
>
> **In the fell clutch of circumstance**
> **I have not winced nor cried aloud**
> **Under the bludgeonings of chance**
> **My head is bloody, but unbowed**
>
> **Beyond this place of wrath and tears**
> **Looms but the Horror of the shade,**
> **And yet the menace of the years**
> **Finds and shall find me unafraid.**
>
> **It matters not how strait the gate,**
> **How charged with punishment the scroll,**
> **I am the master of my fate,**
> **I am the captain of my soul.**

    Shortly after returning from Arizona, the board

announced Aetna was selling its Property & Casualty division. This sent shock waves through the industry because Aetna had been in the business since the 1850's and was one of the largest companies. It also stunned the employee population. Although the possibility had been rumored for months, I don't think any of us thought it would actually happen.

    I was a member of the executive team charged with making sale presentations to prospective buyers. While none of us agreed with this decision, as officers of the company, we had a fiduciary responsibility to get the best price we could. To complicate matters even more, the president formed a group with the six top executives, contacted KKR and we proceeded to prepare our own offer to buy the company. We made a $4 billion offer, but the board decided to sell to The Travelers for roughly the same amount.

    The next several months were consumed closing the deal and handling the transition. It was a painful process for those of us who had spent our entire professional lives with Aetna and never planned to work anywhere else. I was offered a position in the Travelers organization but declined. I had gotten to know the leadership pretty well during the transition and knew there was a major difference in leadership styles. They were command and control oriented and proud of it.

    When Aetna's CEO found out I was not going to Travelers, he called me to see if I would return to Aetna to help them with the integration of a new healthcare company they had purchased. I agreed to work for two more years, which would get me to fifty years old, where I could retire, on the condition the company would move me back to Virginia and whatever I did could be done from there. He agreed and I consulted on integration issues for eighteen months, then at the ripe old age of fifty, I retired. I had a wonderful career with Aetna and my only regret is it ended too soon. I could not have imagined how my career would progress when I started in Richmond in 1970, fresh out of college. I'm again reminded of the quote; **"You know you're happy when reality is better than your dreams."**

EPILOGUE

I have often been asked why I retired at such a young age and at the height of my career. It was not a difficult decision. I saw the business world moving in a direction contrary to beliefs I valued most. The single biggest contributor to my success at Aetna was the hard work, dedication, drive, passion and commitment of the thousands of employees I had the privilege to work with over the years. I could not get passionate about downsizing or outsourcing or the devaluing of employees. I knew my limitations and was comfortable with them. For me it was like the popular World War I song; How Ya Gonna Keep em Down on the Farm (After They've Seen Paree)? I had witnessed Paree and nothing else would elicit the passion required for me to be effective. I have watched with dismay the erosion of employee satisfaction, quality and the extinction of customer service. America has the smartest, most productive workers on the planet; they deserve better than they get today.

During my Aetna career, I had the honor and privilege to mentor and coach several people that went on to have very successful careers themselves. One is currently vice-chairman of a major corporation and many are or were vice-presidents of big companies. The principles that worked for me also delivered for them and achieved the same quality results.

I did accomplish my objectives. I became a leader and achieved superior results in several different situations. I provided a good, secure living for my family and was the highest ranking minority in the history of the company when I retired. The **Five P's, Planning, Preparation, Proactivity, Passion and Performance** had delivered in a big way. I developed the Four Traits for great leaders, **Vision, Communication skills, Courage and Vulnerability** and in every unit I led, created the six characteristics of **High Performing Organizations, Trust, Candor, Teamwork, Diversity, Empowerment and**

Accountability.

In 2007 Lee Iacocca, arguably one of the greatest CEO ever, asked, "Where Have All The Leaders Gone," and said that we should be outraged at the lack of leadership that exist in every aspect of American life. I share Mr. Iacocca's concerns. Business leaders must understand employee engagement is critical for success and will only occur with enlightened leadership that promotes and expects a highly participatory corporate culture. I believe this leadership void is the biggest threat to our continued ability to compete in this rapidly growing, fast-pace global marketplace.

We have to realize the decimation of our superior workforce is not in our best interest; that technology is at its best when it is used to enable an engaged workforce and not as a substitute for it. That the long term cost of outsourcing far outweighs the short term benefits. People, not machines, are the answer to the speed and agility necessary to maintain our competitive edge. The innovation and creativity that comes from the collaboration of people, with diverse ideas, who share a sense of ownership in the business, create tremendous value. We have to develop leaders who understand **good technology in the hands of engaged employees is a powerful tool that generates High Performance and High Satisfaction. I did it. You can too.**

The Author is available for Guest appearances

FOR ADDITIONAL COPIES AND INFORMATION CALL
434-378-2140

Alfred L. Austin

    Mr. Austin reminds us that in this fast moving technology driven world, Human Resources are still the main ingredient in High Performing Organizations. He shows how you can achieve extraordinary results, even from humble beginnings if you use his Five P's strategy. His compelling story will inspire you to take control of your own life and realize your dreams. With real life examples he will show you how, "You can get people to do almost anything if your motives are pure, your rationale convincing and sincere and the interaction takes place in an atmosphere of Trust and mutual Respect".